Face Reading
QUICK & EASY

About the Author

Richard Webster has been involved in psychic subjects for most of his life, beginning with the study of palmistry at age nine, and he joined the Theosophical Society at seventeen to further his knowledge. For several years he conducted horoscope parties in people's homes that involved mind reading, crystal ball gazing, and palmistry, and then spent ten years teaching psychic development classes. These classes quickly outgrew Webster's home and were moved to a local community center. At the same time, he held a large number of one-off workshops on astral travel, past-life regressions, and auras. In addition, Webster has been involved in publishing, bookselling, hypnotherapy, and osteopathy. He also made his living at different times as a pianist, magician, palmist, stage hypnotist, and ghostwriter. For some years he wrote daily horoscopes for Radio Pacific, a New Zealand radio station.

Face Reading
QUICK & EASY

Richard Webster

Llewellyn Publications
Woodbury, Minnesota

FIRST EDITION
First Printing, 2012

Book design by Donna Burch
Cover photo © Glow Wellness/Getty Images
Cover design by Adrienne Zimiga
Editing by Connie Hill
Interior illustrations © Mary Ann Zapalac

Llewellyn Publishing is a registered trademark of Llewellyn Worldwide Ltd.

Library of Congress Cataloging-in-Publication Data

Webster, Richard, 1946–
  Face reading : quick & easy / Richard Webster. — 1st ed.
      p.   cm.
  Includes bibliographical references and index.
  ISBN 978-0-7387-3296-1
1. Physiognomy. I. Title.
  BF851.W35   2012
  138--dc23   2012021930

Llewellyn Publications
A Division of Llewellyn Worldwide Ltd.
2143 Wooddale Drive
Woodbury, MN 55125-2989
www.llewellyn.com

Printed in the United States of America

Other Books by Richard Webster

For my good friend
Shayne Thompson,
"King of the Facial Tells"

Contents

It is the common wonder of all men, how among so many millions
of faces, there should be none alike.
—SIR THOMAS BROWNE

Introduction

For many years, I made my living as a magician. As I was frequently asked to perform something when I was out and about, I always carried a few magic tricks that I could perform at any time. One of these involved handing a coin to someone and asking her to place the coin in one of her hands behind her back. She then had to make both hands into fists and hold them in front of her. Once she had done that, I told her I was going to ask her two questions, and she could either lie or tell the truth. I would point at one hand and ask: "Is the coin in this hand?" She would answer yes or no. I would then ask: "When you said no (or yes), were you lying?" I would then tell her which hand the coin was in.

This was a magic trick, and her responses to my questions didn't matter, as I already knew where the coin was. However, after doing this effect for some time, I discovered there was no need for trickery. In almost every case, the person's face told me which hand the coin was in.

This was an exciting revelation. I had been interested in traditional face reading since attending a talk by Laura Rosetree, a well-known face reader, in the late 1980s. However, I hadn't thought of combining people's facial expressions with a face reading. I still occasionally tell people which hand they are holding a coin in, but now I do it genuinely, anywhere, at any time, purely by reading their faces. I hope you'll be able to do this, and much more, by the time you've finished reading this book.

Although you may not know it, you are already an excellent face reader. You can tell if people are happy, sad, indecisive, timid, broadminded, aloof, friendly, caring, trustworthy, or tired by looking at their faces. You are likely to make mistakes occasionally, but most of the time your first, immediate impressions will be correct.

You also notice people's facial features, and make character assessments based on them. Old sayings, such as "don't trust someone who has eyes too close together" or "he has bedroom eyes," have a basis in fact.

My mother never trusted people with beady eyes. She described the eyes of someone who was thinking spiteful thoughts as small, round, dark, malicious, and beady. Agatha Christie expressed this vividly in *Murder on the Orient Express*: "The body—the cage—is everything of the most respectable—but through the bars, the wild animal looks out." [1]

Throughout your life, you've been making rapid and instinctive decisions about everyone you've met. With the help of this book you'll be able to take this several steps further and gain a greater understanding of yourself and others.

This book is in two parts. Part One covers traditional face reading. Part Two covers the art of interpreting the clues provided by subconscious facial expressions. By the time you've finished reading this book, all of your interactions with other people should become smoother and more effective. You'll be able to read people's personalities in their faces, recognize their talents, and see their inner drives and needs. You'll also find you'll gain a much better understanding of yourself. You'll be able to recognize negative qualities and turn them around. You may discover talents that you didn't know you possessed. You'll also find that all your interactions with others will be smoother and easier, as you'll be more tolerant and understanding.

Reading people's faces, and their facial expressions, is no longer a fringe activity that can be ridiculed and dismissed. It's a skill that, once learned, will become extremely useful to you. You'll be able to use it for many purposes, including: gaining insights into someone's personality, determining if someone is lying or telling the truth, gaining rapport, resolving conflicts, and discovering people's inner nature. You'll also be able to discover possibly unknown talents by examining your own face. At the very least, you'll learn more about yourself and appreciate yourself for the miracle that you are.

Keep a mirror close by as you read. One of the best ways to learn is to use your own face as a guide. It is also a good idea to check what you've learned with photographs of people you know well. You'll be surprised at how much you'll learn about yourself and others.

Part One

THE ART OF
FACE READING

There are mystically in our faces certain characters
which carry in them the motto of our souls,
wherein he that cannot read A, B, C may read our natures.
—SIR THOMAS BROWNE

chapter 1

FIRST THINGS FIRST

Although you may not know it, you're an excellent face reader. Ever since you were born you've read, and interpreted, faces. Most of this is done within a few seconds of meeting someone. We all use expressions, such as "an open countenance," "stern face," "highbrow," "pin head," "he looks honest," and "he looks shifty to me." Even something vague, such as "I don't know what it is, but there's something about him I don't like" probably relates to the person's face.

Most of the information that causes us to make these comments is unconscious. People make up to 90 percent of their impression of others within four minutes, and 60 to 80 percent of that is obtained from our face and body language.[1] We decide if someone looks kind, aloof, aggressive, honest, or friendly within moments of first meeting him or her.

However, some people still give credence to old beliefs, such as "people whose eyes are too close together are shifty," and "someone with a large, bulbous nose drinks too much." I remember my grandmother telling me that someone with a mole on his or her right cheek would enjoy a happy and successful life. Success wouldn't come as easily to someone with a mole on his or her left cheek. This person could achieve success, but only after a great deal of hard work and effort. In this book, you'll find out whether or not these old beliefs are true.

The Five Elements

Ancient Chinese astronomers, astrologers, geomancers, doctors, and face readers used the five elements of wood, fire, metal, water, and earth. The interaction of these five elements was believed to have created everything in the universe.

The elements can be arranged in a number of different ways. The productive cycle is creative, and shows that each element is born from the element preceding it: Wood burns and produces Fire. Fire produces Earth. Earth produces Metal. Metal can be liquefied to produce Water. Water nurtures and produces Wood.

Each element has a number of associations, such as a color, season, direction, and usefully, from our point of view, a face type.

Wood

Color: Green

Season: Spring

Direction: East

Face type: Long, slim, and rectangular, but with a broad forehead and indented temples. Straight nose and narrow eyebrows.

Face keyword: Rectangular

Wood is creative, innovative, sociable, and community-minded. People with a Wood face are optimistic, enthusiastic, and always looking ahead. They are logical, well organized, competitive, and disciplined. They enjoy responsibility, and work hard. They also possess leadership potential and feel frustrated whenever they feel hemmed in or limited in any way. They are naturally kind, understanding, and generous.

Fire

Color: Red

Season: Summer

Direction: South

Face type: Wide middle section, with a pointed chin, narrow forehead, and sparkling eyes. Thick hair and eyebrows.

Face keyword: Triangular

Fire warms and cheers, but it can also burn and destroy. People with a Fire face are enthusiastic, courageous, passionate, self-centered, empathic, and restless. This inner restlessness is often revealed by the quick, sometimes nervous, movements of their bodies. Fire people enjoy setting worthwhile goals for themselves. They also enjoy taking risks and need to be constantly active to be happy.

Earth

Color: Brown, yellow

Season: Late summer

Direction: The center

Face type: Large, square or oblong face, with a strong jaw, generous mouth, and full lips. Fleshy ears and nose.

Face keyword: Square

Earth is patient, honest, methodical, and just. People with an Earth face enjoy routine activities, and are reliable, stable, practical, and conscientious. They dislike change and unexpected happenings. They are also sympathetic, patient, thoughtful, grounded, modest, and friendly. They have a tendency to be rigid and stubborn.

Metal

Color: White, gold

Season: Fall

Direction: West

Face type: Oval, with wide upper cheeks, and a large nose. Straight hair. They often have highly expressive eyes.

Face keyword: Oval

Metal symbolizes business, harvest, and success. People with a Metal face are sensitive, idealistic, gracious, and creative. However, they can also be arrogant, outspoken, authoritative, short-tempered, anxious, and disappointed when perfection is not achieved. They rise to positions of authority and responsibility.

Water

Color: Blue, black

Season: Winter

Direction: North

Face type: Round face, broad forehead, large eyes, prominent chin, large ears, and thick hair.

Face keyword: Round

Water can be both gentle (soft rainfall) and violent (a hurricane). People with a Water face are sympathetic, sensitive, flexible, and emotional. They make good counselors, as they enjoy helping others. They can be dreamy, intuitive, tenacious, and mysterious. People with a Water face are adaptable and find it easy to adjust to the ups and downs of life.

Most people are a composite of two or more elements. However, you might know one or two people who have single-element faces. The elements provide the first clue about someone's character.

Of course, as people's faces come in a variety of shapes, few people can be slotted neatly into one element. Consequently, someone might be Wood/Fire, for instance, or Water/Metal, or any other combination of the five elements.

Other Ways to Classify a Face

Over the centuries, physiognomists have come up with a number of different ways to assess faces. Although Western physiognomy began separately, without any input from the East, it also featured a system of five different types of faces.

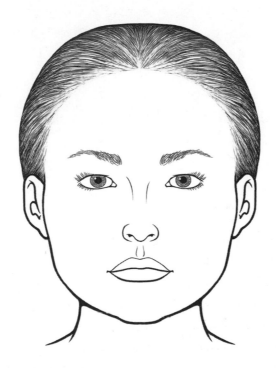

Round

People with rounded faces possess good social skills, and are able to get on with virtually anyone. They are confident, reliable, easy-going, and good-humored. However, they can be impulsive, and frequently act as soon as they've come up with an idea, rather than giving it time to mature. They enjoy all the comforts life has to offer, and are generous with what they have. Although they sometimes need to be motivated, they are shrewd in business and often do well financially. They also do well working for others and generally rise to a position of responsibility. They are modest in their success, and although they enjoy making a profit from a transaction, they seldom desire or receive recognition for what they have achieved.

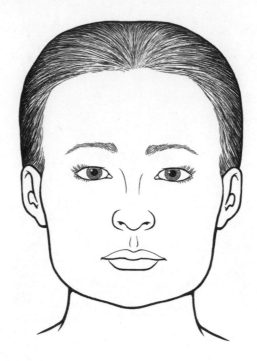

Square and Oblong

People with square or oblong faces are practical, down-to-earth, capable people who can turn their hands to virtually anything. They are determined, patient, and able to motivate others. They achieve success through hard work and persistence. Most of the time, their heads rule their hearts. This explains why they can also be rigid, judgmental, and stubborn.

A true square face occurs when the width at the temple is virtually the same as the width of the jaws. These people have practical minds, and prefer to work without supervision. They enjoy teaching other people how to do things and then giving them the freedom to do it themselves. They often rise to positions of power and prestige.

Many people with oblong faces are high achievers. They are prepared to work hard for what they get and thoroughly enjoy the rewards of their success.

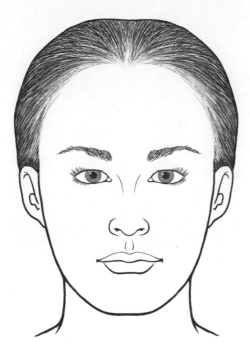

Oval

People with oval faces are caring, considerate, sympathetic, and empathetic. They are logical, and are able to look at problems from all sides. However, they change their minds frequently, making it hard for other people to know what they really think. The ideas they come up with are well considered and beneficial for everyone concerned. They are highly intuitive and able to assess people at a glance. Their main problem is finishing what they start.

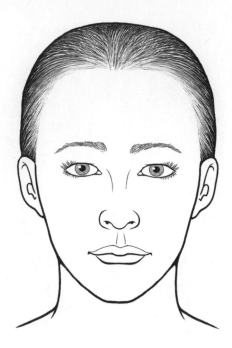

Triangular

People with triangular faces have wide temples and narrow, pointed chins. Their features are pointed and angular. They are curious, possess inquiring minds, and have a wide range of interests. However, they get bored easily, and many interests do not last for long. They have good imaginations and won't hesitate to embroider or exaggerate a story to make it sound better. They prefer to do their own thing, and often find social gatherings uncomfortable and awkward. They have critical natures, which makes it difficult for them to have many true friends. They are ingenious and inquisitive, and this helps them achieve worldly success. Many intellectuals belong to this group, but most triangular-faced people are not in academic fields, and use their active brains in a variety of areas where their analytical skills can be put to good use.

If the chin is narrow, but not pointed, the person will be affectionate, gentle, and creative. He or she will often be highly intelligent and have a studious nature.

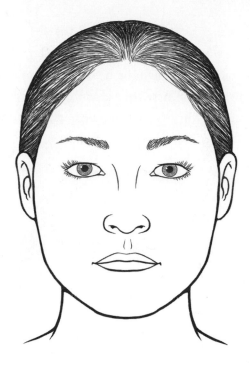

Conical

People with conical faces have wide temples and a square or rounded chin. Their faces are not as angular as triangular faces. They are intelligent, creative, and cheerful. They are tactful and get on well with others, but find it hard to stand up for themselves. Consequently, they frequently give in, rather than argue the case for what they really believe. They are good administrators, but are conservative and dislike change. They enjoy their own company and often have solitary hobbies.

Composite Faces

Sometimes it's easy to classify someone as round or oblong. At other times it can be difficult. It might be hard, for instance, to categorize someone as round or oval. Someone else might be triangular or conical. In these instances, the people combine qualities from the different shapes they belong to. Here are some examples.

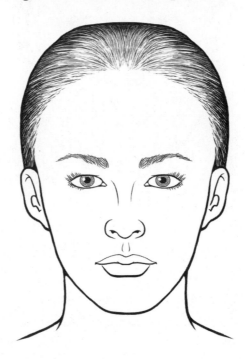

Round-Triangular

People in this category have wide temples that slope inward to create a triangular shape. However, instead of a pointed chin, the jowls and chin are rounded.

These people have the mentality of the triangular type, coupled with the business acumen of the round. They are confident and positive but sometimes fail to act, as they are sensual people who can be easily sidetracked.

This category also includes people with round upper faces and a pointed chin. These people are quick-witted, ingenious, and quick to act. They do well in business.

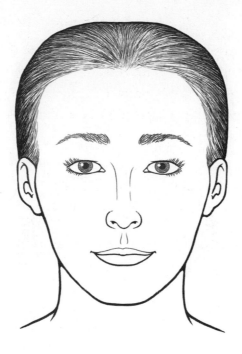

Triangular-Square

People in this category have wide temples, narrowing sides of their faces, and square jaws. These people can come up with good ideas and immediately act on them. They are versatile and are easily able to jump from one activity to another. They are shrewd and often pick trends before they become popular.

This category also includes people with square faces, and narrow, pointed chins. They are quick-thinking people who learn from experience. They frequently do well in life, as they make clear, logical plans, and then act upon them.

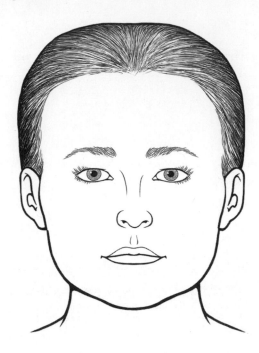

Square-Round

People in this category have square or oblong faces, with a distinct widening and rounding at the jowls and chin. They are happy, sociable, active people who make the most of their opportunities. Although they get on well with almost everyone, they are always looking for ways to benefit themselves.

This category also includes people with a round face that finishes with a square jaw. These people are tolerant, generous, easy-going, and forgiving. They are often lazy but will act quickly, and work hard when they see a potential business opportunity.

Three Types of Faces

Many face readers reduce the number of face types to three: square, round, and triangular.

Square

Square faces belong to confident people who can influence and lead others. They are practical, determined, and possess great will power. They are often interested in sports.

Round

Round-faced people are outgoing, sociable, enthusiastic, and adaptable. They enjoy the best of everything and follow their interests with great passion and energy.

Triangular

Triangular faces belong to people who are thinkers and dreamers. At different times, they can be one or the other. They have good imaginations, and are often found in creative-type occupations. They lack confidence early on in life, and this sometimes holds them back.

It is best to choose one of these systems, and learn it thoroughly. Once you have it mastered, experiment with the other ways to classify face types. By the time you've done this, you'll be able to classify one person as having an oval face, a second person as having a Water face, and a third person as having a triangular face.

The Back of the Head

There are two factors that are determined by an examination of the back of the head: the shape of the head, and whether it is broad or narrow.

Head Shapes

There are three main head shapes: round, square, and egg-shaped.

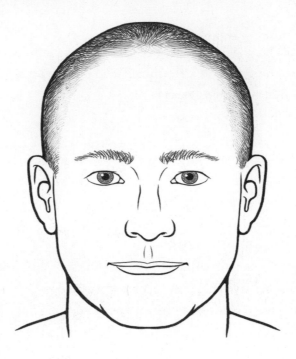

Round

People with a semi-circular curve at the top of their heads are confident in their abilities and willing to take calculated risks at times. They
get on well with others but can be aggressive when roused.

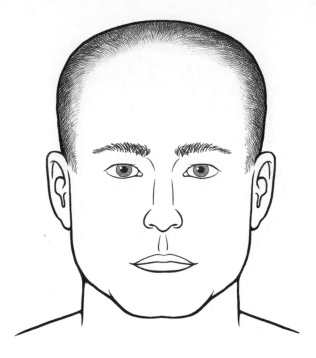

Square

People with a flat top to their heads, and reasonably straight sides, fit into this category. These people are cautious, careful, and reliable. They think carefully before acting, but once their minds have been made up, they act decisively.

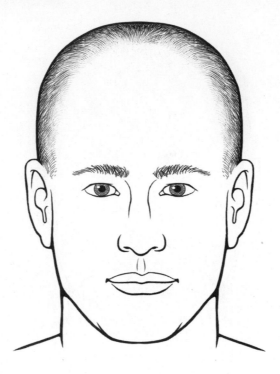

Egg-Shaped

People with a conical head that resembles the pointed end of an egg belong to this category. They are intuitive, adaptable, tactful, discreet, and changeable. They adapt and make the most of any situation they find themselves within. They usually have a high sense of their own self-importance.

Broad or Narrow

It takes practice to determine if a head is broad or narrow. Most heads are average, which means the interpretations for the head shapes (round, square, and egg-shaped) will fit them well. If the height and width are approximately similar, the head is said to be broad. People with narrow heads appear to have long faces because the height (from the jaw to the top of the head) is noticeably longer than the width.

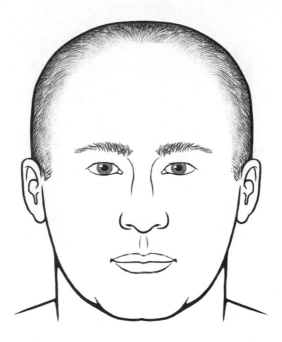

Broad Head

Broadness provides drive, ambition, and a willingness to do anything necessary to succeed. These people project an image of confidence, no matter what they might be feeling inside.

People with broad, or wide, heads are quick-thinking, outgoing, authoritative, and restless. They have a need to be busy, and enjoy taking charge. They prefer the overall picture and tend to ignore the finer details.

People with round-shaped, broad heads are naturally forceful and direct. Usually they can moderate this by using their natural charm. However, some fail to do this and tend to override and bully others.

People with square-shaped, broad heads are demanding, difficult, controlling, and antagonistic. They enjoy giving orders but dislike receiving them.

People with egg-shaped, broad heads are deep thinkers who enjoy learning everything they can about anything that interests them.

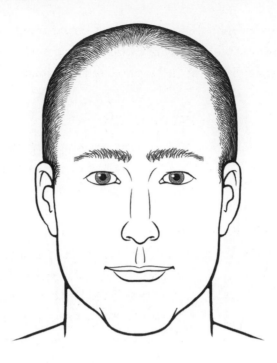

Narrow Head

Narrowness is a sign of moderation and self-control. Many narrow-headed people are introverts, and most avoid the public eye. Consequently, they often struggle to reach positions of seniority and authority, as their demeanor sometimes holds them back. Although there is nothing they can do about the shape of their heads, they can help their chances of promotion by paying attention to their posture and wearing clothing that indicates power and success.

People with round-shaped, narrow heads tend to worry about what other people think, and this holds them back from achieving their goals. These people gain confidence through experience and are often reluctant to try something new or unfamiliar.

People with square-shaped, narrow heads find it hard to say no and can be imposed upon by others. They are overly cautious and hold themselves back.

People with egg-shaped, narrow heads hold themselves back from great achievement but experience enormous delight when they accomplish small goals that boost their sense of self-importance.

Divisions of the Face

The face can be looked at in a variety of ways. The two most commonly used methods are to divide the face in two vertically and into three horizontally.

The Two Sides of the Face

The two sides of the face represent the ancient Chinese concept of yin-yang. Yin and yang are the balancing and harmonizing factors in the universe. They are opposite energies, and neither can exist without the other. Night and day is an example. If there was no night, there could be no day. Rather than defining yin and yang, lists of opposites were often used to demonstrate them. Examples include: up and down, male and female, alive and dead, tall and short, black and white. The popular yin-yang symbol is a circle containing a white and a black tadpole-like shape. Inside the white (yang) tadpole is a black eye (yin), and inside the black tadpole (yin) there is a white eye (yang), to show that there is yin inside every yang, and yang inside every yin.

The left side of your face indicates your innermost, private self. It shows how you relate to family and close friends. It also reveals your father's influence on your life. The right side of your face reveals your outer personality, or the face you show to the world. This is the face that people see when they meet you for the first time, or have dealings with you at work. It also shows the influence your mother had on your life.

Nowadays, it is probably more correct to say that the left side of your face indicates the major male influence in your life as you were growing up, while the right side indicates the major female influence.

Most faces are not symmetrical when you mentally split them into two vertically. The eyes may vary in size and shape, the nose may lean more toward one side, one ear may be higher, lower, larger or more prominent than the other, and so on. A friend of mine has a prominent cheekbone on his left side and a less obvious cheekbone on the right side. This is an indication of the strong influence his father had on him when he was growing up.

It is easier to notice the differences in each half by looking at pairs of features, such as the eyes, eyebrows, ears, nostrils, and cheekbones.

As well as being able to determine which traits came from each parent, you'll be able to tell the traits the person wants to display to the world (right side), and the traits that are intended to be private (left side).

Until you've learned all the basics of face reading, you may find it easier to read one side of a person's face, to avoid becoming confused with the contradictions you'll find on almost everyone's face. Consequently, if you're reading for a friend or looking at the face of someone you're thinking about entering into a relationship with, you should examine the left side of his or her face. When looking at the face of a work or business colleague, you should look at the right side of his or her face.

The Three Zones

The face can also be divided into three horizontal sections, usually known as zones. However, this cannot be determined until the person's face stops growing, which is about the age of twenty. If you look at the head of a baby you'll notice that the forehead is by far the most dominant part of the face. Gradually, the middle section containing the nose develops, and finally, in early adulthood, the third section (chin, lips, and mouth) becomes fully developed.

The first zone starts at the hairline, or where the hairline would have been in the case of people with receding hairlines. It finishes immediately above the eyebrows. This section is called the "Analytical Zone."

The second zone starts at the top of the eyebrows and finishes immediately below the nose. This section is called the Ambition Zone.

The third zone starts immediately below the nose, and finishes at the bottom of the chin. It is called the Practical Zone. It is also sometimes called the Grounding Zone.

With most people, one zone is larger than the others. As the difference can be extremely slight, it takes practice to determine which zone it is. However, once you've got into the way of looking at faces in this way, you'll find it becomes automatic.

You'll also encounter people with two zones noticeably larger than the third zone.

You'll also occasionally come across people who have all three zones about the same size. Oddly enough, this is a rare combination.

You'll be able to determine which is your strongest zone by looking in a mirror while placing one forefinger at the top of your eyebrows, and the other at the bottom of your nose. You can also measure the different zones using your thumb and forefinger.

Analytical Zone

People with strong analytical zones like to think first before making a decision. Consequently, it is sometimes called the intellectual zone. These people enjoy evaluating, analyzing, and studying. Most decisions are made logically. They also love ideas, enjoy abstract thinking, and possess a good imagination.

In traditional Chinese physiognomy, a large analytical zone indicates a happy childhood and early adulthood (from birth to twenty-eight).

Ambition Zone

People with strong ambition zones keep their feet on the ground, and do not get carried away with flights of fancy. They utilize a pragmatic approach, and are prepared to work hard to improve their situations. They also enjoy the rewards of success, such as money, status, and the ability to enjoy the best of everything. In their earlier years, they can be adventurous, but become more cautious as they get older. People with a strong ambition zone often have an air of dignity and nobleness, which is easily recognized by others.

In traditional Chinese physiognomy, a large ambition zone indicates success in the middle years (from twenty-nine to fifty). Vladimir Putin is a good example of someone with a dominant ambition zone.

Practical Zone

People with a strong practical zone are well grounded and keep their feet firmly on the ground. They feel secure, capable, and in control. Although people with strong practical zones may deny any interest in psychic matters, they regularly rely on their gut feelings when making decisions. These people also feel secure in their sexuality. In fact, this area is sometimes known as the "Earth Zone," as these people have a physical, passionate, and sensual approach to life.

In traditional Chinese physiognomy, a large practical zone indicates a happy old age (fifty-one to seventy-five). Obviously, seventy-five is not considered particularly old nowadays, but in ancient China it was an advanced age. Consequently, the practical zone is considered to represent the person's life from fifty-one until he or she dies. Old age is considered a fortunate time in China, and elderly people are respected and looked up to. This is also the period in which these people achieve their greatest successes. The president of Zimbabwe, Robert Mugabe, is a good example of someone with a large practical zone.

No zone is better than any other. Someone with all three zones equal in size will be well balanced and easy to get along with. However, someone who has one zone more predominant than the others possesses an area of strength that can be used for his or her advantage.

Let's assume you're thinking about relocating to another city. If you have a strong analytical zone, you'll research the new city carefully. You'll study the demographics of different neighborhoods, check the crime statistics, examine potential work opportunities, reputation and quality of schools, and availability of any services you require. Before deciding on the part of town you'll live in, you'll examine the availability of shops, public transportation, and the length of your daily commute. After you've done this, you'll interview several realtors, and choose the one who gives you the most detailed information.

Now we'll assume you have a strong ambition zone. You'll investigate work opportunities, and determine if the relocation will be worthwhile financially. You'll look at the cost of housing, and decide if you should buy or rent a house. You'll look at self-employment and investment opportunities. Before buying a particular house, you'll examine the costs of heating and air conditioning.

Finally, let's assume you have a strong practical zone. Once you've made the decision to relocate, you'll want to get on with it, and make the move. You'll probably have a gut feeling about the part of town you want to live in, and you'll choose a house in the area in the same way. As you have a practical approach, you'll quickly determine what needs to be done to the house to make it suitable for you and your family. You'll act quickly, possibly looking at the house in the morning and buying it on the same day.

My wife and I bought the house we live in from a Chinese realtor who'd lived in the country for only a few years. He had been the company's top salesman every year since he began. We enjoyed dealing with him, as he was patient and anything but pushy. He seemed to have a genuine desire to help us find the perfect house for our needs. When I asked him what he did to become the top salesman every year, he laughed and told me he studied people's faces. He was prepared to provide every bit of detail that the analytical zone buyer needed. He provided all the financial and materialistic information that the ambition zone buyer required. Finally, he was ready to write up a contract on the spot when he saw the right signals on the face of the practical zone buyer. The "hidden edge" this realtor possessed was probably worth hundreds of thousands of dollars a year to him.

Spheres of Influence

The face is also divided into eight areas that govern various aspects of life.

1. FOREHEAD—CAREER: The forehead relates to the person's working life. A smooth forehead is a sign of success in one's career. Any deformities indicate problems and difficulties in the person's career, and are a sign of slow progress.

2. BETWEEN THE EYEBROWS—AMBITION: The space between the eyebrows reveals the amount of drive and ambition the person has. It should be wide, smooth, and clear. If this area is narrow, the person will be sociable, but will lack great ambition. The wider this area is, the more easy-going, generous, and forgiving the person will be.

3. IMMEDIATELY ABOVE THE EYEBROWS—FAMILY: This area should be smooth, clear, and free of any marks. This area relates to home and family life, the love between different family members, and the influence the family has on the person. It also relates to inheritances.

4. OUTER TIPS OF THE EYES—MARRIAGE: The outer tips of both eyes should be clear and free from any abnormalities. This area relates to a successful and harmonious long-term relationship.

5. THE CHEEKS—SOCIETY: The cheeks reveal how the person relates to society, and friends in general. If the cheekbones are clearly marked, the person will make strong, long-lasting friendships, and relate well with society as a whole.

6. THE NOSE—HEALTH, MONEY, AND LUCK: The area between the eyes, which includes the bridge of the nose, relates to health. The person will enjoy good health if this area is wide. If this area is narrow, the person will experience many minor health concerns. The rest of the nose is concerned with money and good luck. Consequently, there may be truth in the old saying: "he has a nose for money." Any deformities indicate financial ups and downs, and fluctuations in good fortune. Clearly visible, open nostrils indicate bad luck in financial matters. The Chinese have a saying that the nose is similar to a moneybox. If it's wide at the top, plenty of money can come in. A large nose can hold more money than a small nose. Large, open nostrils allow the money to fall out and escape.

7. BETWEEN MOUTH AND NOSE—COMFORT. THE CHIN —HOME: The areas above and below the mouth relate to the person's home life. If these areas are smooth, the person will enjoy a stable, comfortable, and happy home life. Any defects indicate problems in these areas.

8. RIGHT AND LEFT SIDES OF THE FOREHEAD—TRAVEL: These areas reveal how much travel the person does, and what he or she gains from experiencing life in different cultures.

Now that we've looked at the face as a whole, we'll start looking at individual features, starting with the ears.

Show me your ear and I will tell you who you are,
where you come from, and where you are going.
—DR. AMÉDÉE JOUX

chapter 2

THE EARS

Ears come in an amazing array of shapes and sizes. They cannot be interpreted solely from the front. Even if they stick out like elephant ears, they need to be examined from the side.

Traditionally, large ears were considered a sign of wisdom and intelligence. The ears are the only part of the face that continues to grow throughout life, which is why many old people have extremely large ears.

In traditional Chinese face reading, the ears relate to the kidneys, and to the years from conception to thirteen.

Large and Small Ears

Some ears are obviously large, while others appear to be tiny. It can sometimes be difficult to determine if someone's ears are large or normal in size, as they need to be compared with the length of the person's face. Consequently, ears that might appear large on one face might be a normal size on someone else's face.

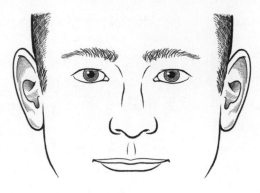

Large Ears

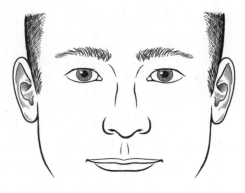

Small Ears

The ears are considered large if four or fewer ear lengths can fit inside the person's face, measuring it from the chin to the top of the forehead. Five or six ear lengths are considered normal length, while anything more than that is considered small.

In China, large ears were considered a sign of longevity and good luck, especially if they also had large and fleshy lobes. Shou Xing, the Chinese god of longevity, is always depicted with extremely long ears. Large ears were also a sign that the person had plenty of stamina and energy. Buddha had extremely large ear lobes, and these were considered a sign of his spiritual development and elevated status.

People with large ears are natural leaders and are willing to take charge whenever necessary. They are outgoing, sociable, and sensual.

They are also prepared to take risks that would frighten someone with smaller ears.

People with average-sized ears are reasonably outgoing. They are also careful, and take risks only after serious thought.

People with small ears are thoughtful, cautious, introverted, and quietly ambitious.

People who have ears that are noticeably different in size to each other have more than their share of ups and downs as they go through life. Interestingly, many people with different-sized ears achieve success late in life, after they've learned their lessons the hard way.

As well as length, ears can be wide or narrow. People with wide ears are prepared to take a calculated risk. People with narrow ears are much more cautious, and evaluate the situation carefully before acting.

If the top half of the ear is larger or broader than the bottom half, the person will have a good brain and an excellent memory. If the middle third of the ear is wider than the top or bottom sections, the person will have a creative and inventive mind. If the bottom half of the ear is long, broad, and fleshy, the person will be sympathetic and compassionate.

Ear Shape

Once you start looking at people's ears, you'll discover how varied they can be. However, the external shape of the ear can usually be described as round or square.

If the ears are round or rounded, the person will be outgoing, sociable, positive, reliable, and imaginative. Frédéric Chopin (1810–1849), the Polish composer and pianist, had round ears.

If the ears are squarish on the tops, sides, and lobes, the person will be shrewd, insightful, quick thinking, and able to do several things at the same time.

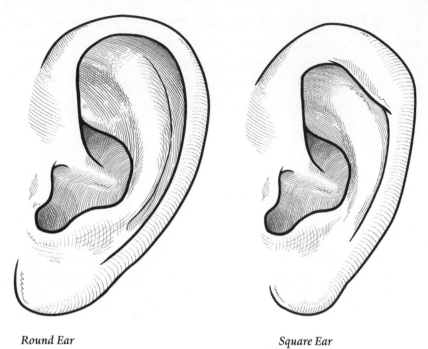

Round Ear   Square Ear

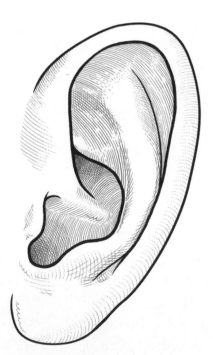

Rounded Pointed Ear

You will occasionally find ears that rise to a rounded point at the top. People who have these are probably tired of being compared to Mr. Spock. People with ears of this sort are mysterious, secretive, and good talkers. Although they're friendly, they keep a lot back, and it usually takes a long time to get to know them well.

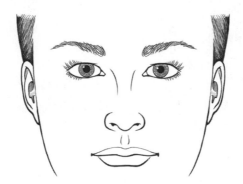

Flat Ears

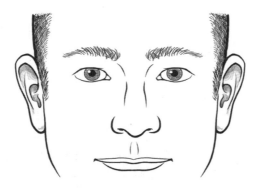

Forward Facing Ears

Flat or Forward Facing

When I'm doing face readings, I'm constantly amazed at the number of people who ask me if their ears stick out. Apparently, many people are sensitive about their ears.

In fact, it's a good thing to have ears that stick out. These people are independent and don't like being told what to do. They can be stubborn. They're non-conformists and prefer to make up their own minds, rather than accept too much on trust. They also tend to attract money. People with these ears usually hear only what they want to hear. Incidentally, face readers usually describe stick-out ears as "forward facing." I assume this is to make people with stick-out ears feel better about themselves. In my experience, most people with stick-out ears feel much more positive about them after learning what they mean. Prince Charles (1948–), heir to the British throne, is a good example of someone with forward-facing ears.

People with ears that hug the side of their head are good listeners. They're also tactful, sensitive, forgiving, and able to fit in to any type of situation.

Ear Setting

Average ears are set between the tip of the nose and the outer end of the eyebrows. High-set ears are situated higher than the tip of the nose and the ends of the eyebrows. Low-set ears are situated lower than the ends of the eyebrows and the tip of the nose.

Long-eared people will have ears that start above the outer end of the eyebrow, and finish lower than the tip of the nose.

People with ears that are set between the tip of their nose and the outer ends of their eyebrows are like most people. This is not very helpful for a face reader, as it denotes an average sort of life.

People with ears that are high-set keep their feet firmly on the ground. They are good, steady, reliable workers, and have a down-to-earth, common-sense approach to life. However, if their ears are set well above the eyebrows, they'll be ambitious, persistent, and ultimately successful.

People with ears that are low-set are idealistic, conversational, intelligent, and easy to get on with. They always need something to look forward to. In China, people with low-set ears were believed to be upper

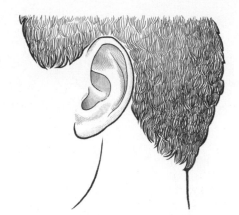

High-Set Ears

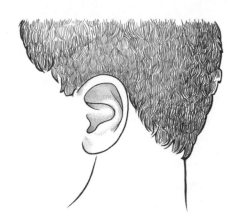

Low-Set Ears

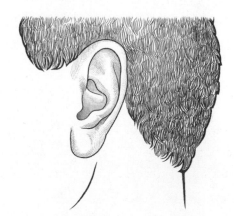

Long Ears

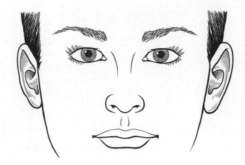

Uneven Ears

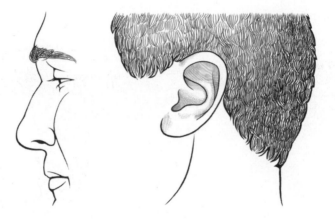

Tilted Ears

class. Although this is no longer the case, people with low-set ears are believed to have come from a privileged background.

A few people have one ear noticeably higher than the other. Almost always, the right ear is higher than the left. This is a sign that the person experienced some form of emotional detachment from his or her mother during the growing-up years.

Ears are usually slightly tilted, with the top of the ear situated farther back than the bottom. If the angle of the tilt is extreme, the person will be rigid and try to control others. He or she will also have an exaggerated sense of his or her own importance.

Parts of the Ear

There are three parts of the ear that need to be examined when giving a face reading: the helix, conch, and earlobes. The tragus is not read.

The Helix

The helix is the outer rim of the ear. As you know, the helix can be rounded or square. People with a rounded helix enjoy mental stimulation. They possess plenty of energy, and enjoy having a good time. They also have plenty of common sense, and this will be noticeable at a very early age.

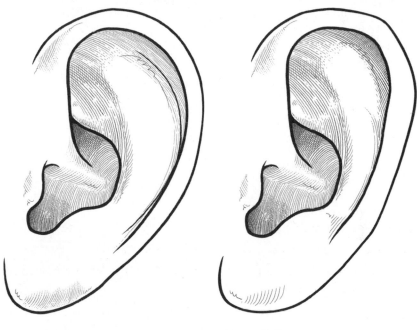

Round Helix   *Square Helix*

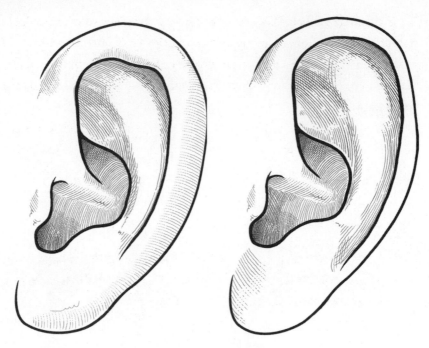

Thick Helix   Thin Helix

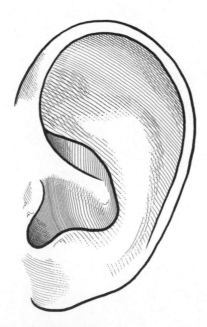

Extremely Thin Helix

If the helix is thick, the person will have a tendency to overindulge in sensuous activities and enjoy all the luxuries he or she can afford.

If the helix is thin, the person will be enthusiastic, impulsive, and extroverted. He or she will have a tendency toward aggression when stymied by others.

If the helix is extremely thin, or even nonexistent, the person will be concerned for humanity as a whole. This person will withdraw into him- or herself when faced with too much stress or pressure. He or she will enjoy quiet times to think, ponder, and regain lost energy.

The Conch

The conch is the shell-like inner circle of the ear. If both the helix and conch are equally well defined, the person will possess the necessary ability and motivation to achieve ultimate success.

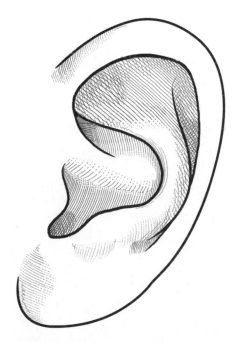

Prominent Conch

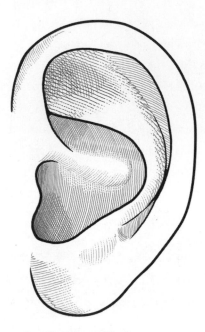

Less Prominent Conch

If the conch is more prominent than the helix, the person will possess enormous stamina, and be able to take a project all the way from idea to completion.

If the conch is less noticeable than the helix, the person will need to push him- or herself to achieve success in life.

The Tragus

The tragus is the flap that protects the ear hole. It lies between the conch and the cheek. It does not play a role in face reading, though it has become a popular part of the ear for ear piercing.

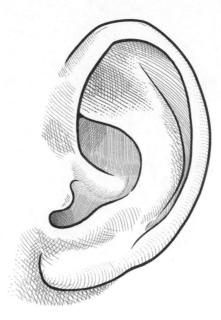

Tragus

The Earlobes

The earlobes are found at the base of the ear. They can either be attached to the side of the head, or separated from the side of the head. People with earlobes that are attached to the side of their heads have a strong connection with their family. People with earlobes that are slightly separated from the side of their heads are more independent in outlook and do not need the close support of their immediate family.

Earlobes can also be long or short. People with long earlobes plan ahead, and enjoy putting their ideas into practice. In China, long earlobes are a sign of wealth, wisdom, and longevity. This is because people who plan well ahead are likely do well financially in the long term.

People with small earlobes live very much in the present and don't enjoy planning too far ahead. They have little patience and express their emotions freely.

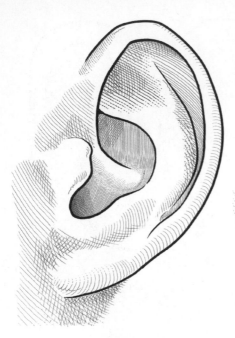

Attached Earlobe

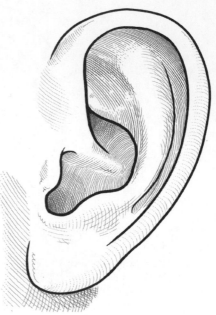

Detached Earlobe

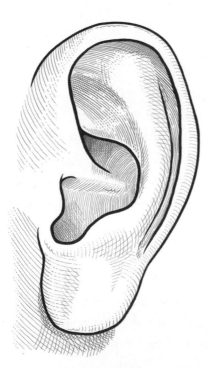

Long Earlobe

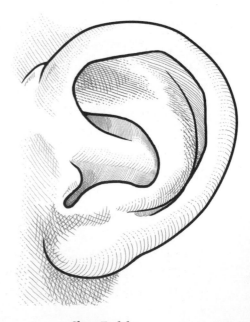

Short Earlobe

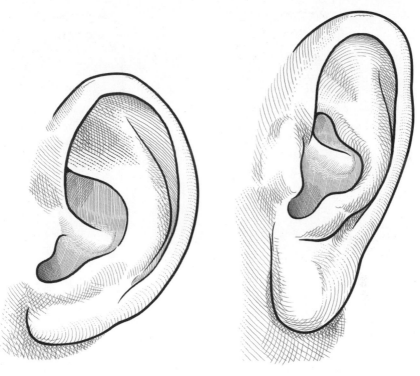

Small Earlobe   *Fleshy Earlobe*

Some earlobes are so short as to be almost nonexistent. People who have these are romantics at heart. They also have excellent imaginations.

People with fleshy earlobes have a strong sensual side to their nature. This is especially the case if they are long as well as fleshy. These people also, according to Chinese tradition, do well financially. In China there is a saying that goes: "The fatter the earlobe, the fatter the purse."

Hair Inside the Ear

Many people have a small growth of hair at the entrance of the ear hole. This needs to be compared with the rest of the person, as some people are naturally hairier than others. If the amount of hair in the ear is excessive when compared to the rest of the body, the person will be filling up his or her life with senseless activities, and wasting the talents he or she has been given.

In the next chapter, we'll examine what some people consider the most important single aspect of face reading: the eyebrows and eyes.

The eyes of men converse as much as their tongues, with the
advantage that the ocular dialect needs no dictionary,
but is understood the world over.
—RALPH WALDO EMERSON

chapter 3

THE EYEBROWS
AND EYES

The Eyebrows

Eyebrows are one of the first things you'll notice when you take up physiognomy. This is fortunate, as a great deal of information can be gained from the eyebrows alone.

In ancient China, it was considered auspicious to have long, thick, and smooth eyebrows that were set well above the eyes. Conversely, inauspicious eyebrows were those that were short, thin, unruly, and set close to the eyes. Fortunately, this reveals only a small part of the picture.

Eyebrow reading was given a special section in *Arcandam Peritissimus*, a famous sixteenth-century book on divination. In this book you can read: "The eyebrows large show the man to be arrogant, and without shame ... the eyebrows which descend crooked on the side of the nose declare the man to be witty in naughty things." [1]

Actors and comedians have always known the value of eyebrows. Groucho Marx raised and lowered his (fake) eyebrows to make people laugh. This became his signature gesture. In the same way, Roger Moore, the British actor, regularly conveyed his feelings by raising a single eyebrow.

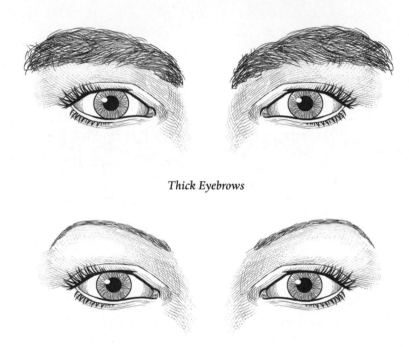

Thick Eyebrows

Thin Eyebrows

Thick or Thin

Years ago, a professional salesman told me that he always looked at people's eyebrows, because they told him how he should approach and deal with potential customers to improve his likelihood of making a sale. I was skeptical, until I saw him in action.

If someone's eyebrows were thick, he would give them a wealth of information about his product. If the eyebrows were thin, he'd give a brief overall summary, and wait for questions, rather than risk losing the sale by telling the person too much all at once.

Even though he hadn't studied face reading, he was correct. People with thick eyebrows enjoy details, and are able to involve themselves in several tasks simultaneously. They are passionate about what they are doing. They love their families and are generous with their loved ones.

People with thin eyebrows are just as intelligent, but prefer doing one thing at a time. They are also more even-tempered and less passionate about their interests than people with full, thick eyebrows.

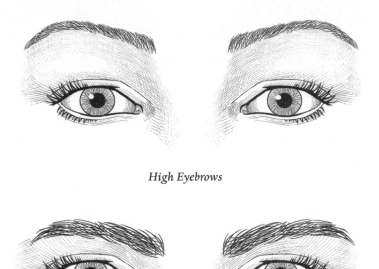

High Eyebrows

Low Eyebrows

High or Low

In traditional Chinese physiognomy, people with eyebrows that were low-set and close to the eyes were said to be ambitious, impatient, and willing to help others. They find it easy to get on well with others, as they're open and friendly.

People with eyebrows that are so close to the eyes they almost appear to be pressing on them are impatient, erratic, easily annoyed, and inclined to fidget. Adolf Hitler (1889–1945), the German dictator, is a good example of someone with eyebrows set extremely close to the eyes.

People with high-set eyebrows are said to be aloof and slightly detached. However, they are also tolerant, generous, and easy to get along with. I used to think the detached and aloof associations probably came about because people with high-set eyebrows can look as if they've raised them deliberately and are questioning something.

However, that was before I chatted with a friend of mine who runs a dating agency. One day she phoned me to say she'd made an amazing discovery. She told me that several men clients had complained that some of the women she had introduced them to were cold and standoffish. She noticed that all of these women had eyebrows that were set well above the eyes. She started paying attention to her clients' eyebrows, and found that men with high eyebrows related well with women with high eyebrows. Likewise, men with low eyebrows got on well with women who had low eyebrows. My friend had discovered independently something that Chinese face readers had known for thousands of years.

Eyebrows that are joined, creating a single line, belong to people who enjoy provoking others, and frequently find themselves in trouble as a result. Fortunately, most of these people learn to modify their behavior as they mature. I've met several people who found life became much easier once they'd plucked the middle hairs. I'm not normally in favor of making deliberate changes to your face, but I do make an exception for people with connected eyebrows.

You will sometimes see people with eyebrows of different heights. These people are overly sensitive, and difficult to get along with.

In traditional Chinese face reading, the wider the gap between the eyes and eyebrows, the happier one's life would be. People with a wide gap between their eyes and eyebrows are able to ask for, and receive, help from others. People with a small gap between their eyes and eyebrows seldom receive this sort of help, and need to work hard to achieve their goals.

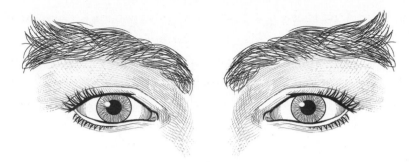

Long Eyebrows

Long or Short

Average length eyebrows extend from one side of the eye to the other. Eyebrows that do not reach the outer corner of the eye are said to be short, and eyebrows that extend beyond the outer corner of the eye are long.

People with long eyebrows get along well with their family and friends. They probably had a happy home and family life while they were growing up, and work hard to make sure everyone in their immediate circle is happy and contented. They also remain in regular contact with their friends. They appreciate beauty, and enjoy having some beautiful objects in their home.

If their eyebrows are thick as well as long, they'll be generous with their time and money. They'll have strong emotions, and are prepared to stand up for what they believe is right. If their eyebrows are bushy, as well as long and thick, they'll be inclined to be stubborn, especially concerning matters that are important to them.

People with short eyebrows see themselves as independent, and find it hard to ask others for help and support. This probably relates to difficulties with other children in the family when they were growing up.

A few people have eyebrows that are so sparse, they can sometimes be difficult to see. These people are quiet, gentle, indecisive, and shy.

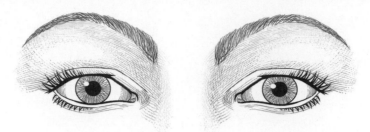

Curved Eyebrows

Curved Eyebrows

People with curved eyebrows are friendly, open, well balanced, stable, and passionate, especially if the eyebrows are also thin. People with eyebrows that are curved and thick are also friendly and passionate, but can sometimes fall victim to their own strong emotions.

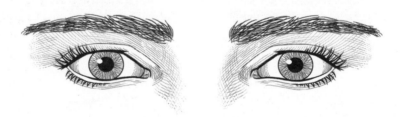

Straight Eyebrows

Straight Eyebrows

Eyebrows usually curve, but sometimes you'll find eyebrows that are set in an almost straight line. People with straight eyebrows are ambitious, conscientious, and business-minded. They enjoy setting goals, and achieving them.

They find it hard to give and receive love, and can appear cold and unaffectionate to others. They need understanding partners who can help them discover their true feelings.

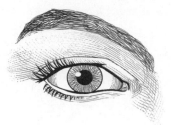

Upward Sloping Eyebrows

Upward Sloping Eyebrows

Upward sloping eyebrows are lowest at the nose end, and rise upward over the outer edge of the eyes. People with eyebrows of this sort are quick to recognize and seize opportunities that other people overlook. They are ambitious, active, hard working, and impatient. However, they have a tendency to slowly lose interest in their careers, hobbies, and other projects over a period of time. Sadly, this can sometimes mean relationships and friendships, too.

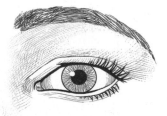

Downward Sloping Eyebrows

Downward Sloping Eyebrows

Downward sloping eyebrows are highest at the bridge of the nose, and slope downward over the outer edge of the eye. People with eyebrows of this type are considerate, responsible, and caring. They work well with others, and are happiest when surrounded by loved ones and friends. People with downward sloping eyebrows are the opposite to people with upward sloping eyebrows, as they become more attached to their hobbies, interests, friends, and relationships as time goes on.

Short Eyebrows

Short Eyebrows

People with short eyebrows are impatient, short tempered, and impulsive. They are inclined to act before thinking, and this causes many problems in their lives. As they mature, most of them gradually learn patience, and this makes their lives easier.

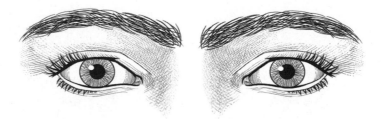

Eyebrows Close Together

Eyebrows Close Together

It has always been considered a negative sign if the inner ends of the eyebrows touch, or are close together. For some reason, eyebrows that are too close together tend to repel others, making it hard for these people to receive help and advice from others. These people take offense easily, and find it hard to forgive others. Former Soviet leader Leonid Brezhnev (1906–1982) had eyebrows that were joined together.

Women with eyebrows that are too close together have usually plucked them. Men with this type of eyebrow will find their path through life becomes smoother when they shave or pluck their eyebrows above the bridge of the nose.

The area between the eyebrows relates to ambition, and ideally this area should be wide and smooth. Consequently, people with eyebrows too close together increase their potential for success once they've plucked their eyebrows in the area above their nose.

The Eyes

The eyes are the most revealing part of the face. Everyone knows the popular saying, "eyes are the windows to the soul." Without knowing anything about face reading, the average person could look into the eyes of a friend and know if he or she was happy, sad, upset, defeated, or exhausted. Most people can tell if someone is happy to see them by the way his or her eyes open wide.

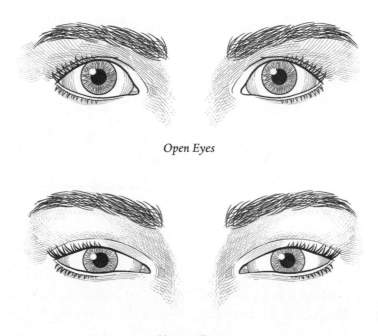

Open Eyes

Narrow Eyes

Open and Narrow

When people's eyes are open wide, they're receptive, emotional, and expressive. If they're excited, and dying to tell someone something, you can guarantee their eyes will be open wide. Their eyes will also shine with the energy of their life force. Conversely, when people narrow their eyes, they are watchful, wary, calculating, and suspicious. People who habitually narrow their eyes are cautious and skeptical.

Large and Small

People with large eyes are intelligent, imaginative, and able to express their feelings freely. They are friendly, affectionate, and inclined to take others at face value. People with large eyes are usually considered extremely attractive. Luciano Pavarotti (1935–2007), the Italian opera singer, had large and expressive eyes.

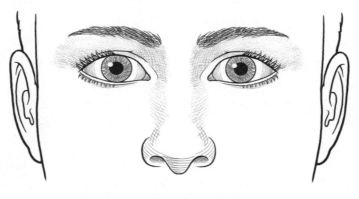

Large Eyes

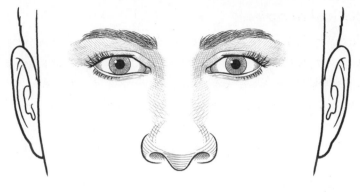

Small Eyes

People with small eyes are more conservative with their emotions, and find it hard to express their innermost feelings. They often find it hard to understand the more theatrical approach of large-eyed people. People with extremely small eyes are materialistic and self-centered.

Bright and Soft

People with bright eyes are enthusiastic, energetic, fun loving, and need to be busy. People with soft eyes are often described as dreamers, as they spend a great deal of time in their imaginations. They have a tendency to be idealistic, and can easily be let down by others.

Bright Eyes

Soft Eyes

Setting

The average distance between two eyes is the length of an eye. If the eyes are set farther apart than that, they are said to be wide-set. If they are closer than one eye length they are said to be close-set.

People with wide-set eyes are able to see the whole situation at a glance. They are ambitious, but often find it hard to finish what they start. They have retentive memories, and possess a natural, innocent charm that makes them seem younger than their years. They have many interests, and enjoy discussing them with others. They're also broad-minded, and hard to shock.

People with close-set eyes are sociable, friendly, and usually have a wide circle of friends. They are analytical, accurate, and good with details. They work best in careers that utilize their concentration skills. They generally change careers at least once during their working lives.

It takes time to get to know people with deep-set eyes. Their mysterious, reserved, and secretive natures appear charming at first, but can become frustrating to people close to them. They find it hard to express their innermost feelings. They are normally late starters, which means they don't usually find the right careers and partners until they're in their thirties.

Average-Set Eyes

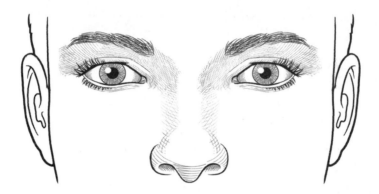

Wide-Set Eyes

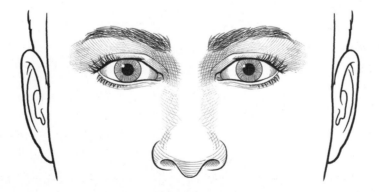

Close-Set Eyes

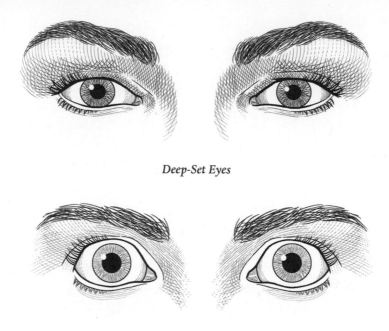

Deep-Set Eyes

Bulging Eyes

People with bulging eyes are exhibitionists who often say outrageous things for the sake of attention. They are enthusiastic, curious, and often impulsive. A comedian friend of mine has bulging eyes, which he jokes about on stage. His act is a series of outrageous observations about his everyday life, and how frequently he is misunderstood.

Corners Curving Upward

If the corners of the eyes curve upward at the outer ends, there are two possibilities, depending on the person's gender.

This is a sign of jealousy and suspicion in a woman. She'll have problems expressing her innermost feelings. Despite this, she'll be open, honest, and genuine in her everyday dealings with others.

Eyes with upward curving corners have a more positive reading for men. It's a sign of hard work, reliability, and a good sense of humor. Men with eyes of this sort enjoy close relationships with women, and are faithful and devoted once they settle down.

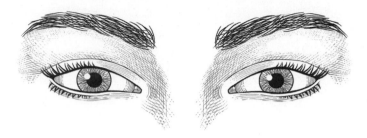

Eye Corners Curving Up

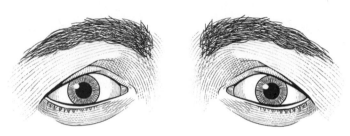

Eye Corners Curving Down

Corners Curving Downward

People with eyes that have corners pointing downward are open and friendly. They have a strong sense of self-interest, and tend to think of themselves first.

Sharp Corners

People with sharp corners at the outer end of their eyes are good at sensing financial opportunities. However, they find it hard to hang on to money once they have it. Consequently, their fortunes vary as they go through life.

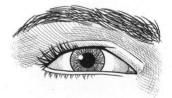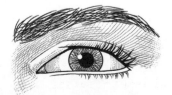

Sharp Eye Corners

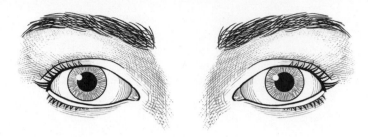

Rounded Eye Corners

Rounded Corners

In face reading, eyes with rounded corners are the most favorable. People with this characteristic are loyal, kind, and devoted to their family and friends. Although they may not necessarily be the life and soul of a party, they are always popular with the special people in their lives.

Curved or Straight Upper Eyelids

People who have curved upper eyelids need something exciting to look forward to. These people remain young at heart, as they're always planning their next adventure. These people are also natural humanitarians, and enjoy helping others.

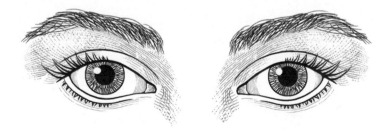

Curved Upper Eyelid

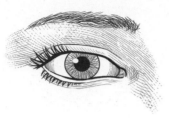

Straight Upper Eyelid

People who have straight upper eyelids look after themselves and have little interest in the welfare of others.

Curved or Straight Lower Eyelids

People who have curved lower eyelids are prepared to make a stand for what they believe is right. However, they are primarily self-centered, and have no interest in the concerns or beliefs of others.

Curved Lower Eyelid

Straight Lower Eyelid

People who have straight lower eyelids are often taken advantage of by others, as they are willing to put other people's needs ahead of theirs. They enjoy careers that involve caring for others, such as teaching or medicine.

Eye Slant

Eye slant is determined by looking at the corners of the eyes and noticing if the outer corner is higher or lower than the inner corner. Most people have eyes with corners at the same level.

People whose outer corner of their eyes is higher than the inner one are enthusiastic, positive, ambitious, and intelligent. They're several jumps ahead of most people when it comes to finding new opportunities. These eyes are sometimes called "cat's eyes."

People with the outer corner of their eyes lower than the inner one are kind, generous, modest, and even-tempered. They have a strong desire to help others, and may need to be reminded that their own dreams and ambitions are just as important as those of anyone else.

Level Eye Slant

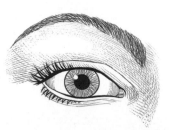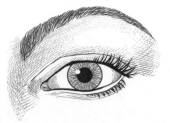

Outer Eye Slant

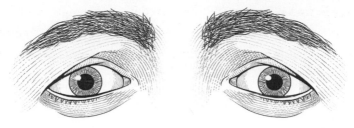

Inner Eye Slant

Crow's Feet

The fine wrinkles that radiate from the outer corners of the eyes are called "crow's feet." They appear as people age, and are considered a positive sign, as they show that the person can see and appreciate the overall picture. This person instinctively knows what is going on around him or her.

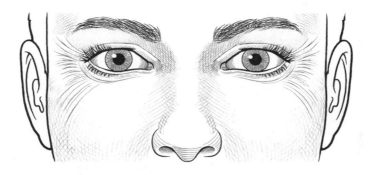

Crow's Feet

Stress

Stress can be seen clearly in the eyes. When you look at your eyes in a mirror, you'll see white (the sclera) on both sides of the iris. Ideally, you should not see the whites above or below the iris. It's a sign of stress when this is visible.

If white is visible above the iris you'll be feeling anxious, nervous, and overly sensitive.

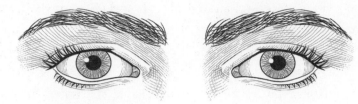

Whites Visible below Iris

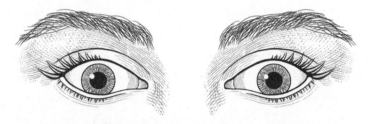

Whites Visible above Iris

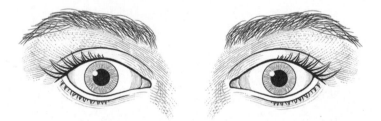

Whites Visible above and below Iris

If white is visible below the iris you'll have become overloaded with stress, strain, and pressure. This could make you anxious, short-tempered, and—in extreme cases—violent.

It is extremely rare to see white both above and below the iris. This means the person is suffering so much stress that he or she is in danger of becoming mentally unbalanced.

Fortunately, if the person takes active steps to reduce the degree of stress, the eyes will reflect that by returning to normal.

When I had a bookstore many years ago, one of my regular customers had eyes with the whites visible both above and below the irises. He was a pleasant man to deal with, but frequently when he was browsing around the store he'd become agitated and have a noisy argument with himself, yelling at an imaginary person in a man's voice, and answering in a female voice. These outbursts would last about a minute, and then he'd return to his usual, charming self again, as if nothing had happened. After these episodes, he appeared to have no memory of the outburst. He used to come into my store at least once a week, but suddenly stopped coming in. When he reappeared, about three months later, the whites were no longer visible above and below his irises, and his strange outbursts never reoccurred. Presumably, he had been receiving treatment for the incredible amount of stress he'd been under.

In the next chapter we'll look at the most prominent feature on the face: the nose.

A beautiful nose denotes an extraordinary character.
—JOHANN KASPAR LAVATER

chapter 4

THE NOSE

In ancient China, a large nose was considered extremely beneficial, as it denoted power, ambition, and wealth. The interpretation is similar today, but the size of the nose needs to be compared with the size of the face, as well as the other features on it. A nose that might be considered large on one person's face may appear small on the face of someone else.

The association with drive, energy, ambition, and power came about because the nose relates to the Metal element in Chinese face reading.

A well-developed nose is generally considered to indicate someone with a strong character. This person would also have plenty of persistence, drive, and ambition. Napoleon Bonaparte (1769–1821) was interested in physiognomy, and is reputed to have said: "Give me a man with a good allowance of nose. When I want any good head work done, I choose a man with a long nose." [1]

As a large nose is related to worldly success, I advise everyone considering a "nose job" to make sure they think about it carefully first. This is because a nose reduction reduces the person's personal power and influence.

People with large noses experience life to the full. Consequently, they sometimes have more than their share of emotional ups and downs. These highs and lows are often self-inflicted.

Large noses relate to power and success. People with smaller noses are not as preoccupied with power and achievement. This doesn't mean they can't become leaders. However, leadership does not come as naturally to them as it does to people with larger noses. (Other factors need to be looked at as well. A prominent jaw and/or well-developed cheekbones can also indicate a leader.)

People with small noses are fun loving, and get along well with others. They enjoy being part of a group, and seldom seek the limelight. They are often shy and reserved. Consequently, it can take time to get to know them well.

There is a common misconception about Jewish noses. People tend to think that these are large, convex, and arched. However, a research study in 1952 of 2,836 male and 1,284 female Jews in New York showed that 57 percent of the males had flat noses, 14 percent concave, 6.4 percent flared, and only 22.3 percent convex.[2]

Long and Short

Aristocratic noses are invariably long. However, it doesn't necessarily mean you're descended from aristocracy if your nose is long. The face reading interpretation of a long nose is someone who is ambitious, forthright, and has good common sense. People with long noses are responsible, and have a strong sense of what's right and wrong. They enjoy planning out an entire project, and following it through from start to finish. However, they can also be extremely stubborn, and tend to take life very seriously.

If your nose is short, you'll be a hard worker, who sometimes finds it hard to say "no" to all the demands other people put on you. You'll be loyal, sensitive, and sympathetic. In China, people with short noses are believed to have ups and downs in fortune.

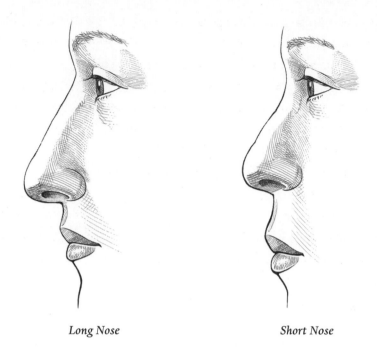

Long Nose   *Short Nose*

Most people have noses that are neither long nor short. This means you're prepared to work hard when it's necessary, but are also prepared to slow down when the pressure is off.

Nose Shapes

Certain types of noses have been named after groups of people. Most people know what shape a Roman nose is, for instance. However, if you went to Rome, you'd find people with every possible type of nose. Two thousand years ago, many aristocratic Romans had this type of nose.

Roman Nose

A Roman nose has a high bridge, or bump, at the top of the nose. If you have this type of nose, you like to take control and be in charge. You are better at giving orders than receiving them. You are also good at managing your money, and keep your finances to yourself.

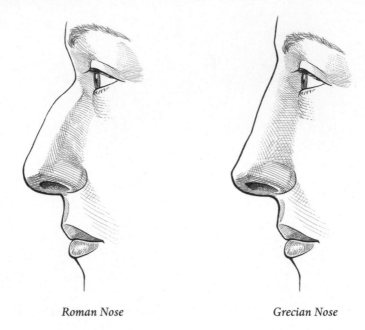

Roman Nose   *Grecian Nose*

Grecian Nose

A Grecian nose is determined by looking at the nose from the side. If the line of the nose continues downwards from the forehead without a dip, it is called a Grecian nose. This type of nose gained its name as many ancient Greek statues depict figures with this type of nose.

This type of nose is seldom seen. People with it have a haughty, imperious approach to life, which they have to modify to function effectively.

Straight Nose

People with a straight nose are disciplined, honest, loyal, reliable, and always appear successful, no matter what their current circumstances happen to be. Interestingly, straight-nosed people frequently achieve the degree of success that they aspire to.

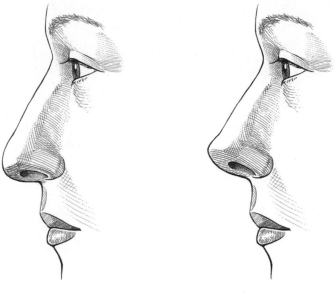

Straight Nose   *Sharp and Pointed Nose*

Sharp and Pointed

People with pointed noses have an inquisitive mind, and want to know all the details about anything that interests them. If the nose points downward, the person has a cool disposition. The more extreme this becomes, the chillier the person will be. Joseph Stalin (1879–1953), former premier of the Soviet Union, had a downward pointing nose. In Chinese physiognomy, someone with a sharp nose that points down markedly is considered unreliable and untrustworthy.

Broad Nose

A broad nose appears wide when looked at from the front, and often appears flat when viewed in profile. People with a broad nose are spontaneous, extravagant, sensual, competent, and sometimes indecisive. They have a wide range of hobbies and interests. They are sociable and get on well with others. Consequently, they make friends

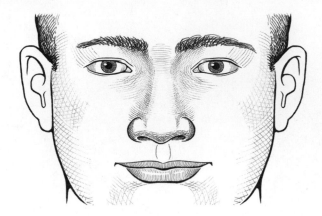

Broad Nose

easily, everywhere they go. They enjoy helping others, and their many friends know they can always rely on them.

Turned-Up Nose

People with turned-up noses that reveal the nostrils are friendly, generous, openhearted, and affectionate. However, as the Chinese think this type of nose looks childish, they consider it a sign of an immature approach to life. It is impossible to make someone with a turned-up nose do something he or she doesn't want to do.

Down-Turned Nose

People with down-turned noses are shrewd and able to assess a situation at a glance. They're also good at discerning the hidden motivations of others.

If the tip of the nose turns downward to partially cover the philtrum, the person's innate shrewdness will extend to financial matters. This person is also careful with money, and manages his or her investments well.

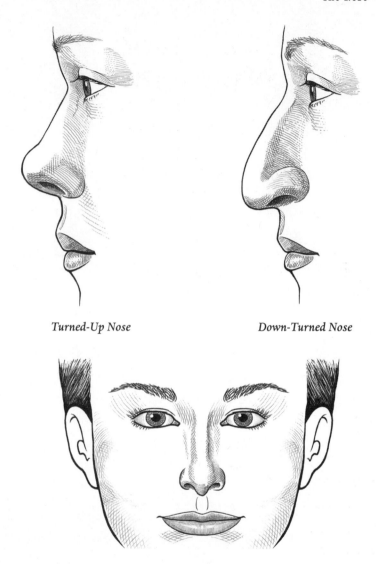

Turned-Up Nose   *Down-Turned Nose*

Bony Nose

Bony and Fleshy

People with bony noses are somewhat ascetic. Their ideals are important to them. They choose careers that they will enjoy, rather than selecting a particular field of work that appears lucrative.

Fleshy Nose

People with fleshy noses enjoy the material comforts and luxuries that life has to offer. I belong to a wine club, and about three quarters of the members have fleshy noses, which reveals their love of good-quality wine.

Nose Tips

Narrow Tip

People with narrow tips to their noses are often accused of being overly harsh and critical. Although this is largely true, it is done with the best of motives, as these people are interested in others, and want to help them achieve their dreams.

Wide Tip

People with wide tips to their noses are tolerant, accepting, and diplomatic. Although they can be critical at times, they usually accept others as they find them, and make no attempt to change them.

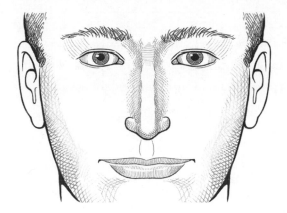

Narrow-Tip Nose

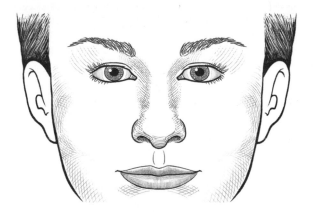

Wide-Tip Nose

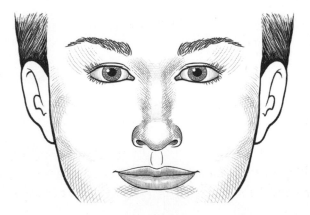

Rounded-Tip Nose

Rounded Tip

People with rounded tips to their noses always buy the best that they can afford. In fact, if they can't afford the quality they desire, they'd rather do without than put up with something that goes against their aesthetic and quality standards.

Fleshy Tip

People with fleshy tips to their noses have good taste, and enjoy good food and quality entertainment. A fleshy tip is sometimes called the "gourmand's tip."

Fleshy-Tip Nose

Split-Tip Nose

Split Tip

People with noses that have a slight groove and appear larger on one side than the other have divided feelings about their love for the good things in life. This sometimes prevents them from letting go and really enjoying themselves. People with a tip of this sort often have big ups and downs in their lives. They have a unique slant on life, which enables them to come up with good ideas.

The Nostrils

Traditionally, the nostrils showed how the person spent his or her money. Today, most face readers look at the nostrils to determine how the person spends his or her energy.

People with large nostrils find it easy to spend money, and also find it a simple matter to put all their energy into a project they believe in. People with large nostrils tend to believe that there is plenty of money around, and they'll receive their share of it whenever it is required.

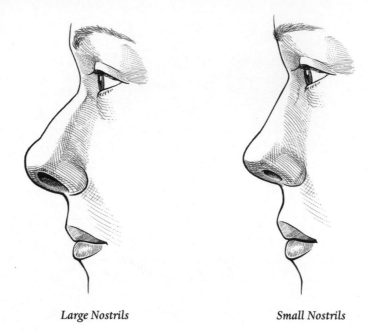

Large Nostrils   *Small Nostrils*

Their tendency to spend freely in the good times can get them into trouble when economic circumstances change. This is especially the case if the person's nostrils are highly visible when you look at him or her face on. They are also independent people who find it hard to ask others for help or advice.

People with small nostrils are able to hold on to both money and energy. They are careful with money matters, and make sure they really need something before buying it. They enjoy finishing one task before starting on the next.

In the next chapter we'll examine the part of the face that is most commonly associated with verbal communication: the mouth.

As are the lips so is the character. Firm lips, firm character;
weak lips, weak and wavering character.
—JOHANN KASPAR LAVATER

chapter 5

THE MOUTH
AND PHILTRUM

The mouth is the most sensual feature on the face. For thousands of years, women have used lipstick to make this feature more attractive and sensuous. Cleopatra (69–30 BCE), Queen of Egypt, used lipstick made from crushed carmine beetles and ants. Mouths are used for kissing, and an examination of someone's lips can reveal what sort of lover he or she would be.

The mouth plays an important part in face reading, as it reveals how generous you are, your feelings about home and loved ones, and your capacity to nurture others. Some portrait artists claim that the person's character can be determined by looking at his or her mouth.[1]

Mouths vary in size, and can be large, medium, or small. This has to be determined by looking at other features on the person's face, because what might be a large mouth on one person may well be smaller on another.

If you find it hard to determine the size of anyone's mouth, draw two imaginary lines downward from the center of the irises of the

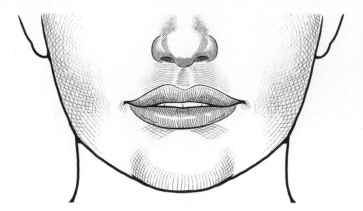

Large Mouth

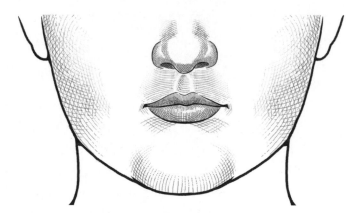

Small Mouth

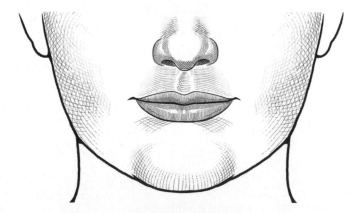

Average Mouth

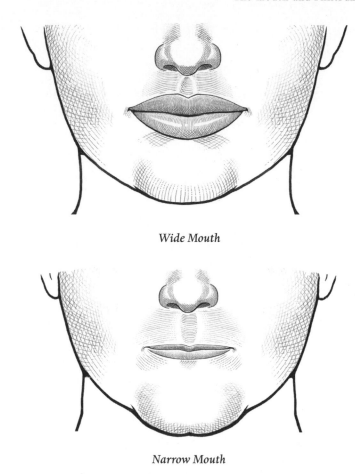

Wide Mouth

Narrow Mouth

person's eyes. If these imaginary lines meet the ends of the person's mouth, he or she will have an average-sized mouth.

People with large mouths are generous and quick to forgive. Home, friends, and family life are important to them. They enjoy having a good time with the people they love. They enjoy sex, and are exciting and passionate lovers. David Letterman, Joan Rivers, and Julia Roberts are good examples of people with large mouths.

People with small mouths are self reliant, and work hard to achieve their goals. They find it harder to maintain relationships than people with large mouths. Their lovemaking is more reserved than people with larger mouths. However, it is said that they have better sex lives. They are easily frustrated, and find it hard to confide in others. They also find it hard to lie successfully. Barbara Walters is a good example of a successful person with a small mouth.

Most people have average mouths. They can handle most people well. They are tolerant, adaptable, and—usually—honest. Johnny Carson was a good example of someone with an average-sized mouth.

People with wide mouths that stretch across their face have positive personalities, and laugh a great deal. Their hearts rule their heads. They crave adventure and excitement, and this can cause problems with most nine-to-five jobs. The best work for them involves plenty of change and variety.

People with narrow mouths are ruled by their heads, not their hearts. They are down-to-earth, practical, serious, and frequently introverted. Interestingly, if these people force themselves to smile and laugh more frequently, their mouths will widen, and they'll enjoy life much more. Life will get better for the people who live with them, too.

Lips

Full Lips

People with full lips are sensual and emotional. They are friendly, sociable, and affectionate. Former president Jimmy Carter has full lips.

If the top lip is fuller than the bottom lip, the person will talk freely about any topic. He or she will also be affectionate, caring, and supportive of others. This person will also have a strong need to be liked and appreciated by others.

If the lower lip is fuller than the top one, the person will be motivated, sensual, and possess a strong ego. However, although this person will be a good communicator, he or she will not enjoy discussing personal or intimate matters.

If the lower lip is much fuller than the top one, the person will love talking and be highly persuasive. Not surprisingly, many of these

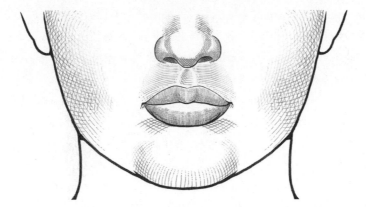

Full Lips

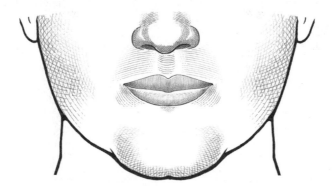

Top Lip Fuller Than Bottom

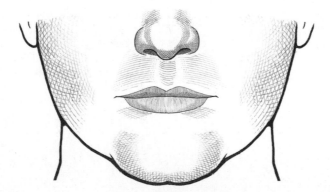

Lower Lip Fuller Than Top

people enjoy working in sales, entertainment, public speaking, teaching, and politics. Larry King, Matt Damon, Margaret Thatcher, and Elvis Presley are three examples of people with very full bottom lips.

Thin Lips

People with thin lips are determined, persistent, and decisive. They are more secretive than people with full lips, and keep their thoughts and feelings under tight control. They express themselves well, as long as it does not include private or personal matters, and are usually good communicators.

It's no accident that many politicians have thin lips. Former president George H. W. Bush is a good example. One of his famous quotes was: "Read my lips: no new taxes."

People with thin lips dislike being teased or made fun of. People with extremely thin lips are emotionally cold, and hard on themselves, as well as others. The negative aspects of extremely narrow lips are softened if the person has a round tip on his or her nose. Thin lips can be an advantage in business where people need to be able to keep secrets.

People with large mouths and thin lips often do very well financially. They can talk easily, but know when to keep quiet or hold back.

If the top lip is noticeably thinner than the bottom lip, the person will be creative, logical, and full of practical ideas. This person will also be reticent, and often keep his or her ideas quiet. He or she has no interest in being in the limelight, and is generally happy to watch what is going on, rather than be the center of attention. This combination is found more frequently on men than on women.

If the top lip is noticeably thicker than the lower lip, the person will need excitement and drama in his or her life. This need is so strong that he or she will create it, if necessary.

If the lower lip is thinner than the top lip, the person will be shy, quiet, and retiring. He or she will have a small group of carefully selected friends, and enjoy spending time with them. He or she will actively avoid crowded or busy environments.

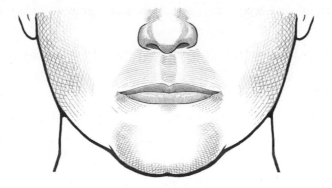

Thin Lips

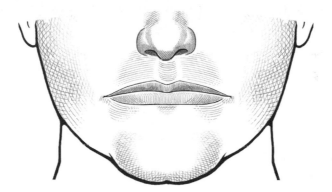

Large Mouth and Thin Lips

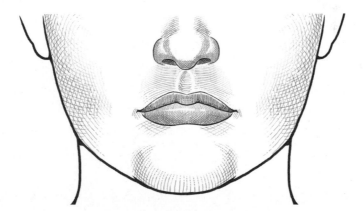

Top Lip Thinner Than Bottom Lip

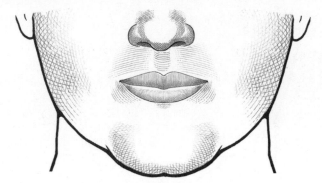

Top Lip Fuller Than Bottom Lip

Protruding Lips

People with a protruding top lip are kind and understanding. They dislike confrontation and find it hard to stand up for themselves. They find it difficult to discuss intimate subjects, but can be extremely sensual with the right partner.

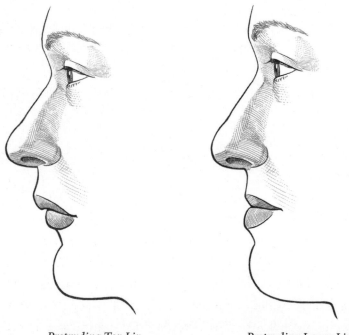

Protruding Top Lip   *Protruding Lower Lip*

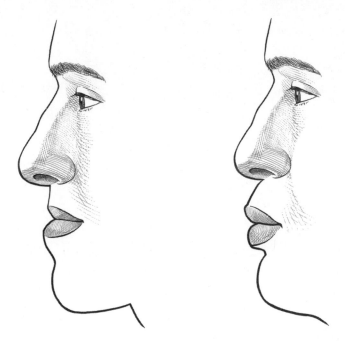

Extremely Protruding Lower Lip   *Both Lips Protruding*

People with protruding lower lips have no problems in standing up for themselves. They're also willing to stand up for, and support, people who are unable to do this for themselves.

However, people with extremely protruding lower lips are impetuous, determined, and tenacious. They are prepared to fight for what they want.

If both lips protrude, the person will be honest and sincere, and possess great integrity.

Upturned and Down-Turned Mouths

People with upturned mouths are considered cheerful, positive, and optimistic. They are mischievous and fun to be around. People with down-turned mouths are considered pessimistic, discouraging, bitter, and lacking in joy. Former US president Richard M. Nixon (1913–1994) had a down-turned mouth. This is exacerbated if the lower lip protrudes beyond the upper lip.

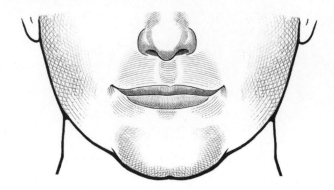

Upturned Mouth

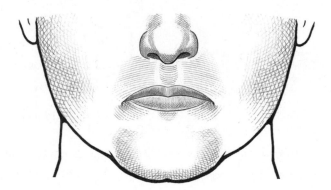

Down-Turned Mouth

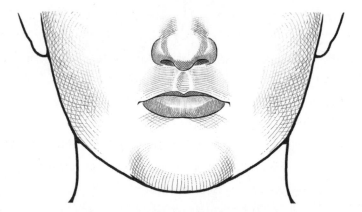

Pouty Mouth

Pouting

People who habitually pout are considered moody. They see themselves as victims, and blame others for everything that goes wrong in their lives.

The Philtrum

The philtrum is a vertical groove that connects the upper lip with the center of the base of the nose. It derives its name from the Greek word, *philtron*, which means "love potion." This is because the ancient Greeks considered the philtrum a powerful erogenous zone. A deep philtrum is a sign of fertility.

There is a charming story about the origin of the philtrum. Archangel Gabriel is considered the archangel of childbirth. As part of her work, she teaches unborn babies their mission in life, and swears them to secrecy. To reinforce this, Gabriel presses her finger on the babies' lips, creating the cleft, or philtrum, under their noses.[2]

In Chinese face reading, the ren zhong, or philtrum, relates to length of life. People with long philtrums can expect to enjoy a longer life than people with short philtrums.

Short Philtrum

If the distance between the upper lip and the base of the nose is short, the philtrum will be short, too. People with short philtrums detest being teased or having people make fun of them.

Long Philtrum

People with long philtrums are the opposite of people with short ones. They enjoy being teased and don't mind being the butt of jokes.

Deep Philtrum

A well-marked, deep philtrum is a sign of creativity and fertility. Many people who work in the arts have prominent philtrums. Of course,

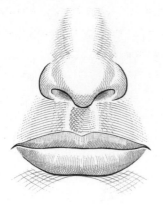

Short Philtrum

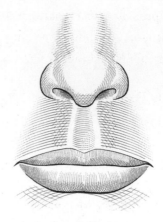

Long Philtrum

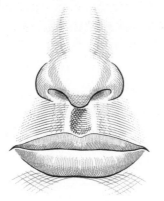

Deep Philtrum

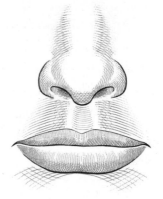

Low Philtrum

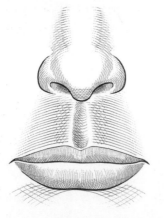

Long, Deep Philtrum

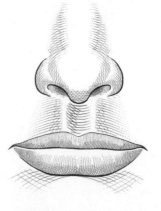

Both Sides Parallel Philtrum

it's possible to be highly creative, and to have a large family, without a well-defined philtrum. The philtrum is just one sign of creativity. A deep philtrum is also a sign of abundant energy.

Low Philtrum

People with philtrums that are almost invisible lack energy and drive. Their success in life depends on them finding a partner with a deep philtrum to push them forward, and to make up for the lack.

Long, Deep Philtrum

People with philtrums that are both long and deep are extremely family-minded. They are happiest in a stable relationship, with children. Children are extremely important to them. If they don't have a family, their nurturing qualities will be evident in some form of creativity.

Parallel on Both Sides

People with philtrums that are the same width from top to bottom are good administrators. They usually rise to a senior position and do well in life. People with philtrums that are parallel on both sides, and are also long and deep, enjoy successful home and family, as well as business, lives.

Wider at the Top

People who have philtrums that are wide at the nose but narrow as they near the lips are said to be most successful in the first half of their lives.

Wider at the Bottom

People with philtrums that widen as they head toward the lips continue to grow in knowledge, wisdom, and wealth as they progress through life. This can also indicate a late marriage.

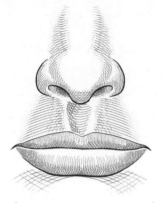

Wider at the Top Philtrum

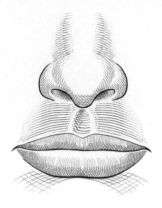

Wider at the Bottom Philtrum

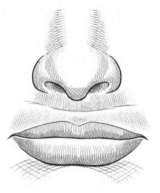

Horizontal Lines on Philtrum

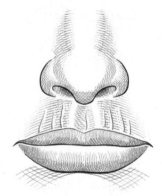

Vertical Lines on Philtrum

Horizontal Lines on the Philtrum

Horizontal lines on the philtrum can indicate problems with the reproductive system. Women with horizontal lines across their philtrums may have lost a child through miscarriage or abortion, had a hysterectomy, or experienced problems during menopause.

Vertical Lines on the Philtrum

A vertical line on the philtrum means one of two things. It can be linked to difficulties in expressing creativity, or it can indicate stress-inducing problems with a child or children.

In the next chapter we'll move up the face to examine the forehead.

I consider the peculiar delineation of the outline and position
of the forehead ... to be the most important of all the things
presented to physiognomical observation.
—JOHANN KASPAR LAVATER

chapter 6

THE FOREHEAD

The forehead plays an important role in face reading. In the first chapter we discussed how it was the first of the three horizontal segments of the face to be fully developed. Like the head, the forehead can also be divided into three sections horizontally. The top section, joining the hairline, is called Heaven. The middle section is called Human, and the bottom section, immediately above the eyes, is called Earth. Ideally, all sections should be broad and evenly domed. However, if one section is more prominent than the others, it provides clues about the talents and skills that have been inherited.

The Forehead

Heaven

The Heaven section of the forehead reveals the qualities that have been inherited from the person's ancestors. These qualities are: a keen intelligence, kindness, generosity, and a love of family.

Human

The Human section of the forehead reveals the qualities that have been inherited from the person's parents. These qualities are: common sense, a down-to-earth approach to life, and strong moral values.

Earth

The Earth section of the forehead reveals the qualities the person has learned from his or her own experiences. These qualities are: a sympathetic ear, a sensual approach, and a strong intuition.

Prominent Forehead

A prominent forehead bulges outward from the hairline. It can be narrow or wide, but always has a distinctive bulge when viewed from the side. People who have a prominent forehead have plenty of energy, and enjoy thinking, analyzing, imagining, and coming up with good ideas. They are persistent, determined, and keen to learn. Albert Einstein is an excellent example of someone with a prominent forehead.

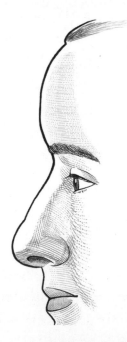

Prominent Forehead

Broad Forehead

Broad Forehead

A broad forehead is wide, and preferably high. People with a broad forehead are open-minded and have a wide range of interests and skills. They prefer the overall picture and tend to get bogged down with details. They normally end up knowing a little bit about everything that interests them, rather than a great deal about one or two subjects. This fascination with new interests keeps them forever young at heart. People with broad foreheads enjoy being in charge. They are born to organize and lead others. Not surprisingly, they are often found in positions of authority where they can put their talents to work. Because they are such good organizers, they are generally successful in what they do. They have a practical and down-to-earth approach to life.

Narrow Forehead

People with narrow foreheads are, in many ways, the opposite of people with broad foreheads. They tend to have a limited range of interests, and are fascinated with the facts and details relating to them. They make excellent researchers, as they want to know everything they can about their chosen topics. They are impractical and sometimes fail to see the forest, as they're so busy looking at individual trees. People with narrow foreheads are unassuming people who tend to conform and don't like to rock the boat. They like to fit in.

Narrow Forehead

High Forehead

They enjoy lengthy discussions with like-minded people. They have no desire to be leaders and are happy to contribute behind the scenes.

High Forehead

People with high foreheads are intelligent, forward looking, generous, and interested in learning. They have retentive memories. The type of learning varies and is determined by the breadth of their foreheads. They enjoy observing, thinking, and coming up with their own conclusions. Charles Dickens (1812–1870), the English author, had a high, broad forehead.

Square Forehead

Low Forehead

Square Forehead

A square forehead is both wide and high. People with a square forehead are intelligent, well organized, and reliable. They carefully examine every aspect of a situation before acting. They are conservative in outlook, and keep both feet firmly on the ground. When necessary, these people can be extremely courageous. They are prepared to work patiently for many years to achieve success.

Low Forehead

People with low foreheads like to think carefully before making a decision. They dislike being hurried. Once they have made a decision, it's extremely hard to make them change their mind. They are patient, conscientious, and persistent.

Flat Forehead

People with foreheads that rise in a straight line upward from the eyebrows are analytical, determined, patient, and modest. They enjoy problems, as they gain pleasure from analyzing and resolving them.

Convex Forehead

People with protruding, convex foreheads are independent, innovative, and frequently charismatic. They get along well with others, and often do well in business.

Concave Forehead

People with sunken, concave foreheads have a limited number of interests, which they follow passionately. Although they are hard workers who sometimes do well financially, they tend to be underrated by others. Because of this, many of them choose occupations that have limited contact with others.

Domed Forehead

People with a forehead that is rounded and broad like a dome have some sort of creative talent. (It's usually easier to see a forehead of this sort from the side.) This doesn't mean they're necessarily working in an artistic field, but they'll certainly make use of their creativity in their work or hobby. Once a year, a man comes to trim the trees in our garden. He has a magnificently domed forehead. He takes pride in his work, and by the time he's finished, every tree is perfectly shaped and pruned. He uses his creativity all day, every day. The architect who drew up the plans for an extension to my daughter's home also has a domed forehead. When I learned to play the piano, my teacher had a domed forehead.

Flat Forehead

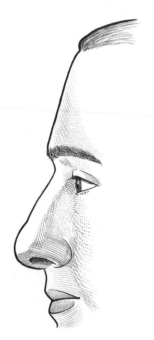

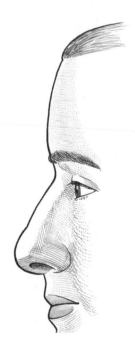

Concave Forehead   *Convex Forehead*

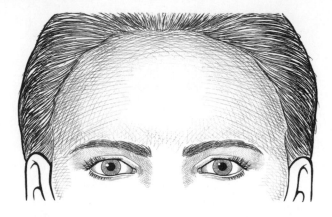

Domed Forehead

Rounded Forehead

Rounded Forehead

A rounded forehead is not as obvious or pronounced as the domed forehead. People with a rounded forehead are inventive people with good imaginations. It's important that their work provide them with sufficient stimulation, as they get bored easily and drift off into a world of their own. They are good daydreamers.

Slanted Forehead

People with a forehead that slants back from the eyebrows are able to come up with unique solutions to problems. They can handle many

Slanted Forehead

tasks at the same time; because of this, however, they often take on too much, and find it hard to finish anything. They prefer to work out their own solutions to problems, and consequently make many mistakes as they progress through life. However, many people with a slanting forehead are entrepreneurs who ultimately become extremely successful.

Markings on the Forehead

The French astrologer and physician Jerome Cardan (1501–1576) developed a system of interpreting the lines on the forehead to determine someone's personality and destiny. He called his system *metoposcopy*, as the Greek word for forehead is *metapon*. He claimed that he could tell if a woman had committed adultery, and if someone was noble in character or a knave. His exhaustive book on the subject,

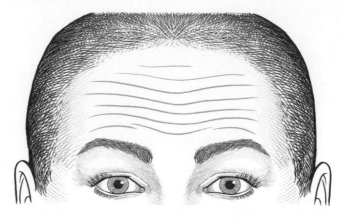

Long, Unbroken Lines on the Forehead

Separated Horizontal Lines on the Forehead

complete with more than 800 illustrations of different character traits, was published in Paris in 1658. It was called *Metoposcopia*.

As he was primarily an astrologer, Jerome Cardan used the seven planets known in his time to name the seven horizontal lines that can be found on a forehead. The line closest to the eyebrows was called the Moon, and the other six lines in ascending order were: Mercury, Venus, the Sun, Mars, Jupiter, and Saturn. In practice, few people have all seven lines. Most people have two, three, or four of them.

Long, unbroken, straight lines that cross the forehead horizontally indicate honesty, openness, and simplicity of the soul. This applies no

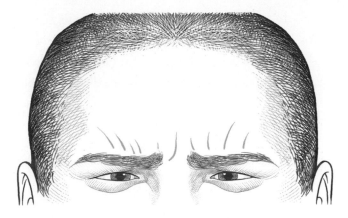

Short Vertical Lines on the Forehead

Vertical and Horizontal Lines on the Forehead

matter which planets the lines correspond to. Three horizontal lines that are well separated show that the person has a strong spiritual side to his or her personality. Short vertical lines indicate sudden, unexpected changes.

Each of these possibilities was illustrated in his book. Consequently, there are illustrations showing a variety of intriguing potential futures. There is an attractive woman who is in danger of a violent death caused by poison, steel, fire, or the plotting of women. There is a woman with six horizontal lines and a single vertical frown line who is clearly an adulteress. According to Jerome Cardan, she would end her days as a beggar. Another illustration shows a man with three distinct crosses on his forehead, showing that he is dissolute, dishonest, and a slave to lust. In addition, he would lose his considerable fortune.

Jerome Cardan's work is remarkable, but with at least 800 different characteristics to learn and memorize, it's not surprising there are few, if any, people practicing metoposcopia today.[1]

Wrinkles on the Forehead

Although few people are prepared to learn all the characteristics that Jerome Cardan wrote about, most face readers pay attention to the horizontal and vertical lines found on the forehead.

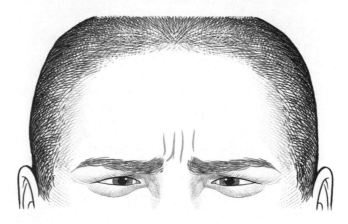

Three or Four Frown Lines

Three or Four Frown Lines

People with three or four frown lines are logical, thoughtful, hard working, and persistent. They like to examine everything carefully before deciding what to do. They proceed only when they are confident in their decision. They are loyal and responsible, and tend to worry about everyone in the family.

One Horizontal Line

One horizontal line is usually found on people with narrow foreheads. Traditionally, it shows that the person had a difficult childhood.

People with one horizontal line are hard workers who often achieve success because of their persistence and determination. They are inclined to look after their own interests, and pay little attention to the needs and desires of others.

Two Horizontal Lines

Two horizontal lines on the forehead relate to the person's relationships with others, and his or her status and reputation.

If the top line is shorter and less obvious than the bottom line, the person will not be able to rely on the support of friends and family in difficult situations.

If both lines are long and deep, the person will relate well with others and would do well in any field that used his or her people skills. This is a sign of popularity.

Three Horizontal Lines

Three horizontal lines are found on the foreheads of worriers. The deeper the lines are, the more worries there have been. However, these people also have retentive memories, and—despite worrying about them first—are good at solving problems. People with three horizontal lines on their foreheads generally do well in life. An old Chinese saying says that a man with three lines on his forehead will become king.

No Horizontal Lines

People with no horizontal lines on their foreheads are seldom taken seriously when they're young, as the lack of lines makes them look like immature young children. However, these people normally start

Two Frown Lines

Angled Frown Lines

to achieve in middle age and continue to look younger than their years well into old age.

One Frown Line

People with one vertical line between their eyebrows are stubborn and persistent. Any success is achieved by hard work, persistence, and the fact that they never give up, no matter what the price may be.

People with one frown line are not very romantic and treat family life as a chore.

Two Frown Lines

People with two vertical lines between the eyebrows are caring, understanding, sympathetic, empathetic people who get on well with virtually everyone. They enjoy marital and family life, and do their best to ensure that everyone they care for is appreciated and treated well.

Angled Frown Lines

People with angled or horizontal lines between their eyebrows tend to overreact, and lose their tempers quickly. This is a sign of immaturity, and many of them gradually moderate their reactions as they suffer from the stress, disharmony, and sadness that accrues when they overreact.

In the next chapter we'll look at the area below the eyes, and between the nose and the ears: the cheeks.

Thus is his cheek the map of days outworn.
—WILLIAM SHAKESPEARE

chapter 7

THE CHEEKS

In China, plump rounded cheeks were considered the most favorable cheeks to have. They were likened to peaches. In the West, high cheekbones have always been appreciated and admired, especially by women.

There are three main types of cheeks, conveniently called Upper, Middle, and Lower. The upper cheeks are from the base of the nose upward; the lower cheeks are from the corners of the mouth downward; and the middle cheeks lie between them.

The Cheeks

Prominent High Cheekbones

People with well-developed, high cheekbones are intelligent, ambitious, independent, and determined. They set high standards, and insist on the best of everything. Former US president Abraham Lincoln (1809–1865) is an excellent example of someone with prominent, high cheekbones. For great success, it's important that both the nose and cheekbones are prominent. This is because they both relate to power and influence.

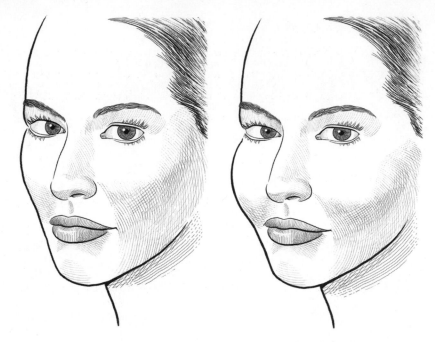

Prominent High Cheekbones   *High Rounded Cheeks*

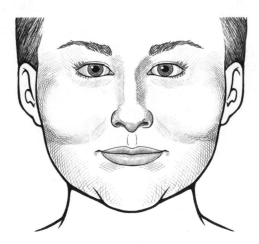

Plump Rounded Cheeks

High Rounded Cheeks

People with rounded cheeks in the upper section are positive, confident, sociable, fun loving, and generous people who enjoy having a good time. In addition, they are motivated to achieve success, and are prepared to work as hard and as long as is necessary to achieve their goals.

Plump Rounded Cheeks

These are the cheeks that the ancient Chinese face readers considered the most propitious. People with plump rounded cheeks are considered powerful, courageous, and strong. Chairman Mao Tse Tung (1893–1976) had plump rounded cheeks. Other good examples are Queen Victoria (1819–1901) and former World Heavyweight Champion boxer Muhammad Ali.

Prominent Upper Cheeks

People with prominent upper cheeks desire power and authority. They're prepared to work hard to reach a level of status and power that suits them. Many choose self-employment, as this puts them in control. Some people with prominent upper cheeks need to learn how to exercise authority, and have a tendency to boss and order others around.

Curved Cheeks

People with curved cheeks are good at getting on with others, but also value quiet times on their own. They enjoy thinking deep thoughts, and make their minds up only after serious contemplation.

Fleshy Cheeks

People with fleshy cheeks are confident, practical, spontaneous, happy people who make the most of every situation. They are sensual, and enjoy sampling all the delights life has to offer.

Prominent Upper Cheeks

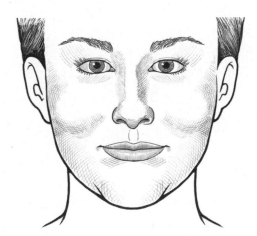

Curved Cheeks

Fleshy Cheeks

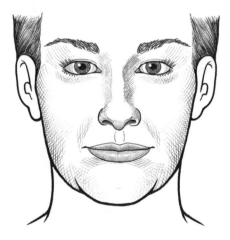

Flat Cheeks

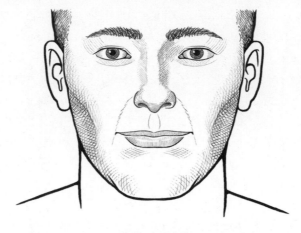

Hollow Cheeks

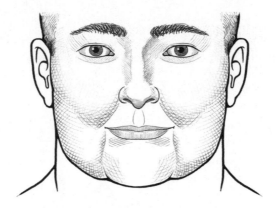

Moneybags Cheeks

Flat Cheeks

People with flat cheeks enjoy their own company, and dislike being told what to do. They work best in situations where they know what has to be done, and are given free rein to accomplish it.

Hollow Cheeks

Hollow cheeks appear sunken or indented. They belong to people who are suffering from stress caused by their emotions or overwork.

They need to be constantly reminded that they are worthwhile, lovable people who have as much right to be here as anyone else.

Grief can also cause hollow cheeks, which return to normal once the grieving process is over.

Moneybags

People with large, plump lower cheeks are said to have "moneybags." When I was very young, I remember my mother telling me about a distant relative who had "enormous moneybags." I wanted to meet her, as I hoped she'd bring her bags of money with her when she visited. Unfortunately, she died before I had a chance to meet her, and we discovered she'd been extremely successful in the stock market.

People with moneybags have the potential to do well financially, as the plumpness gives them the necessary energy to pursue their goals, even in difficult times. When these people are unwell, stressed, or overdoing things, the moneybags retreat—creating jowls that look like empty bags. When they have recuperated and regained their energy, the plumpness returns, and they regain their ability to make money and hang on to it.

The Middle Cheeks

People with full middle cheeks enjoy life, and want to sample as much as possible before their lives are over.

In Chinese medicine, the middle cheeks relate to the lungs. Many cigarette smokers have sunken middle cheeks that reveal how their lungs have been affected by years of smoking.

Dimples

Dimples are usually found in the middle cheeks. People with dimples are charming, flirtatious, and carefree. They are usually popular, but once they settle down, they make a long-term commitment to their partners.

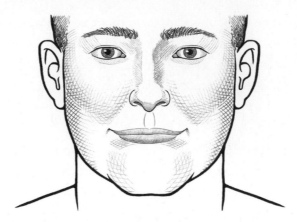

Full Middle Cheeks

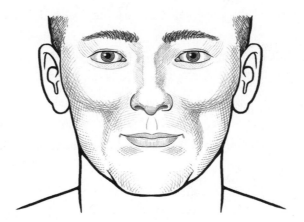

Sunken Middle Cheeks

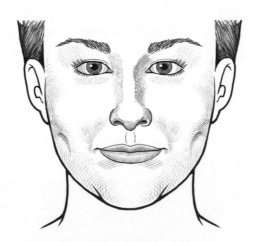

Dimples

Cheek Lines

Cheek Lines

The main cheek lines start at the side of the nose and curve downward beyond each side of the mouth. It's important to have these lines, as people without them are considered incompetent, lazy, and worthless. Fortunately, these lines develop as people age and gain experience in life. Hard work, study, and responsibilities are all said to deepen and extend these lines.

It's considered a negative sign if these lines run into the mouth. People with these lines have difficulty looking after their personal finances, and also have problems with close relationships.

There are also lines that curve beneath the eyes. They start at the inside corner of the eyes, and end on the cheek beyond the outer edge of the eyes. They are usually curved, but can sometimes form a straight line or a semi-circle.

If these two lines are close together at their starting points near the side of the nose, the person will be someone who sets, and acts

Cheek Lines Running into Mouth

Curved Cheek Lines under Eyes

Straight Cheek Lines under Eyes

Semi-circle Cheek Lines under Eyes

Cheek Lines under Eyes that are Close Together

Cheek Lines under Eyes that are Far Apart at Starting Points

upon, worthwhile goals. These could be personal goals, but are just as likely to be goals that could benefit all humanity.

If these two lines are well apart, the person will not be particularly goal-oriented. He or she may set goals at times, but will usually prefer to live life one day at a time.

Blushing

Blushing is a huge cause of embarrassment for many people. Usually, there is a reason for the blush. Feelings of humiliation, guilt, and shame can cause the cheeks to redden. People who are bad liars frequently give themselves away by blushing.

Blushing is a serious problem for people who experience it often. It undermines their confidence, and makes them hesitant and nervous when dealing with others. However, blushing can also be an endearing quality that makes the person seem open, honest, and attractive.

In the next chapter we'll examine the lowermost part of the face: the chin.

A certain lord, neat, and trimly dress'd,
Fresh as a bridegroom; and his chin, new-reap'd,
Show'd like a stubble-land at harvest home.
—WILLIAM SHAKESPEARE

chapter 8

THE JAW AND CHIN

The Jaw

People with strong jaws inspire confidence, and others subconsciously feel safe and protected when in their company. It's not surprising that many politicians have strong jaws. People with strong jaws are opinionated and judgmental, and this can cause problems with friends and family.

People with highly prominent jaws are prepared to stand up and fight for what they believe in. However, they find it hard to accept that other people's ideas may have some validity. Once they learn this, their sense of responsibility, fair play, and justice can take them a long way.

People with narrow jaws are emotional, adaptable, and easy to get on with. They need to make sure that their own needs are being met, as they can be easily swayed by the opinions and suggestions of others.

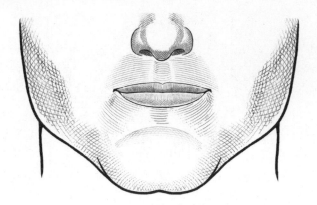

Strong Jaw

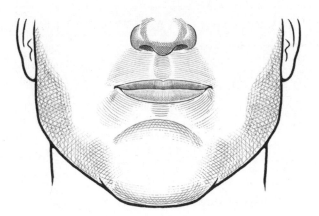

Prominent Jaw

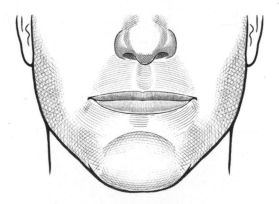

Narrow Jaw

The Chin

The chin has always played an important role in Chinese face reading, as it represents the person's life after the age of sixty. A good chin shows that the person will enjoy a good quality of life in his or her old age.

Greek artists loved protruding chins, and the sculptures of their gods all had strong, powerful chins. The ancient Chinese also liked protruding chins, especially if they were square. They considered this to be the perfect chin for a man.

When someone sets his or her chin, this person is resolving to do something. It's a sign of determination, no matter how small or large the chin may be.

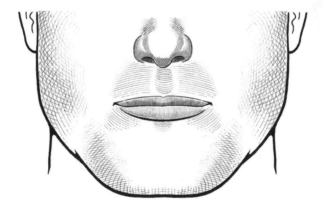

Broad Chin

Broad Chin

People with broad chins are ambitious, confident, determined, and moral. Everything they do is with a purpose in mind. However, they find it hard to express their innermost feelings, and this can cause problems in their most important relationships.

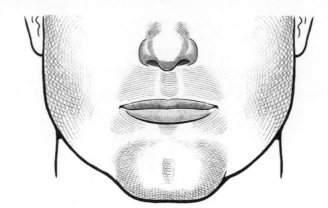

Square Chin

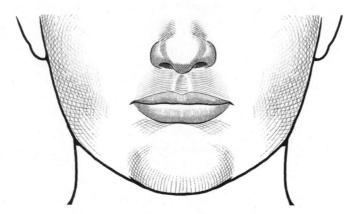

Round Chin

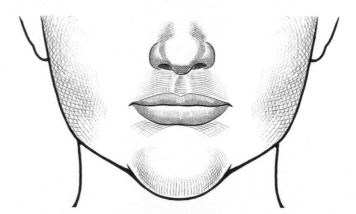

Pointed Chin

Square Chin

People with square chins are energetic, practical, direct, open, and sensible. They are able to look impartially at both sides of a situation, and make up their minds using logic and consideration. If the square chin is overly prominent, the person will be demanding, unyielding, obstinate, and unforgiving. Robert Redford is an example of someone with a square chin.

Round Chin

People with rounded chins are sympathetic, supportive, kind, generous, and family-minded. They are willing to help anyone in need. They tend to be conservative in outlook, and dislike being placed in a leadership role.

Pointed Chin

People with pointed chins are sensitive, friendly, sociable, and fun loving. They need other people around them, and enjoy gossip and knowing what everyone else is up to. They sometimes suffer from indecision. They are stubborn, and have a natural tendency to resist if they feel someone is trying to force them to do something, even if it's something they'd normally enjoy doing.

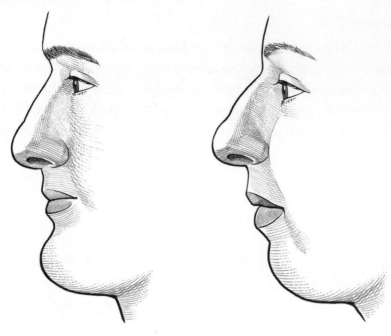

Jutting Chin   *Receding Chin*

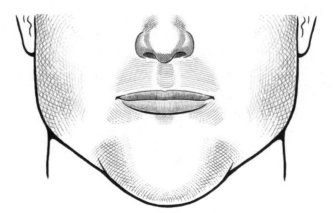

Long Chin

Jutting Chin

People with chins that jut out are forceful, enthusiastic, confident, and sure of themselves. They have tremendous reserves of drive and energy that help them persist until they reach their goals. Jay Leno is an excellent example of someone with a jutting chin. (His chin can also be classified as a long chin.)

Receding Chin

At one time, receding chins were considered weak. However, this is certainly not the case, and people with receding chins are able to stand up for themselves just as well as people with jutting chins. However, they do it in a less confrontational way. People with receding chins enjoy debates and friendly discussions on matters that are important to them. They enjoy quick results, and tend to become impatient when projects drag on longer than expected.

Long Chin

People with long chins are affectionate, loyal, and genuinely concerned about others. Not surprisingly, they make friends easily. They are cooperative and work well with others. They find it easy to express their emotions.

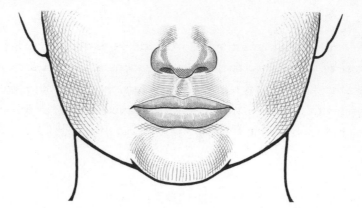

Small Chin

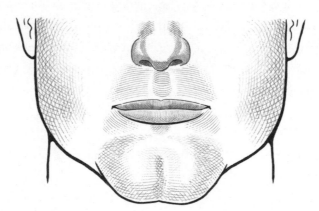

Cleft in Chin

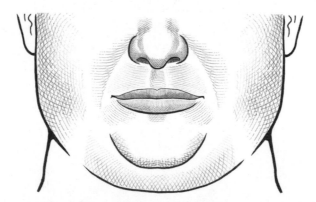

Double Chin

Small Chin

People with small chins need to work harder than others to achieve their goals. Fortunately, they're persistent, single-minded, and determined. They are easily hurt by the comments of others, and, especially early on in life, find it hard to stand up for what they believe in. When mature, they are calm, gentle, easy-going, and prepared to stand up for themselves.

Cleft in the Chin

People with a cleft in their chins enjoy receiving attention, acknowledgment, praise, and credit for their contributions. This constant need for assurance can prove wearing for their partners and work colleagues. They are earnest, and prefer serious conversations to idle chatter. People with cleft chins also possess strong sexual appetites. Humphrey Bogart had a cleft in his chin.

Double Chin

Many people are unhappy that they have a double chin. However, in face reading it's a sign of great happiness in later life. Aristotle wrote that a double chin reveals someone with a "peaceable disposition."[1] Johann Kasper Lavater wrote that a double chin was a sign of an epicure.[2]

In the next chapter we'll examine the hair and the hairline.

Fair tresses man's imperial race insnare,
And beauty draws us with a single hair.
—ALEXANDER POPE

chapter 9

THE HAIR
AND HAIRLINE

Hair plays a minor role in face reading, as it modifies what has been read in the face. Hair comes in a variety of colors and types. Because it's so easy for people to change their hair color, this is not usually read in face reading, but other aspects of the hair are. The exception to this is gray hair. This is a sign of mental maturity, even in someone who has become prematurely gray. As long as other features of the face denote a good character, someone with gray hair will be able to offer good, sound advice.

Types of Hair

Long Hair

People who keep their hair long are practical, capable, levelheaded, and pragmatic. They enjoy discussing, and thinking about, new ideas.

Short Hair

People who keep their hair short are decisive, forceful, vibrant, and energetic. They focus on their goals, and are prepared to work hard to achieve them. Many short-haired people enjoy physical activities.

Shaved Head

It is common today for many balding men to shave off the rest of their head hair. This can sometimes make them appear aggressive. However, exposing the top of the head in this way gives them access to unique ideas, and gives them a more intellectual approach to life. It may also increase their interest in spirituality. Christian, Buddhist, and Hindu monks are frequently tonsured. This is a shaved, bald spot at the top of the head, which helps their connection with the Almighty.

In China, it was considered a sign of exceptional intelligence if a man started losing his hair after the age of fifty. This was especially the case if the hair started receding from the forehead.

Straight or Curly

Before interpreting this quality, you need to determine if the hair is naturally straight or curly. People with straight hair are sympathetic, caring, imaginative, and often introverted. People with curly hair are outgoing, sociable, energetic, and ambitious. In traditional Chinese face reading, people with curly hair were considered shrewd, and were said to possess an unusually strong sex drive. In China, almost everyone has straight hair.

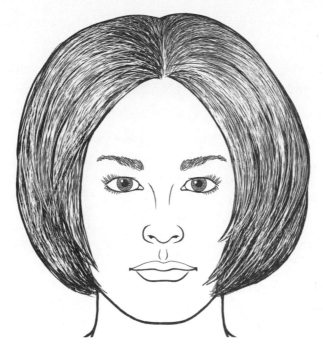

Thick Hair

People with thick hair are active, determined, enthusiastic, and energetic. They enjoy being outdoors, and always need something ahead of them to look forward to.

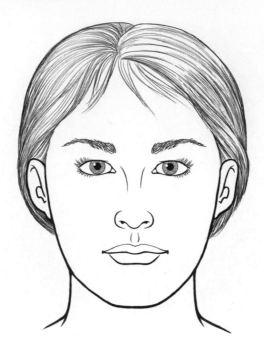

Thin Hair

People with thin hair are sensitive, emotional, and easily hurt. They appear gentle, and can surprise others when they demonstrate their strength and determination.

Dry Hair

In traditional Chinese face reading, dry hair is a sign of financial difficulties in the near future. Fortunately, this can be averted by using a good quality conditioner. You should keep your hair as healthy as possible, as this attracts good luck and good fortune.

The Hairline

Hairlines can be difficult to read—unless they are clearly defined, people's hairstyles make their hairlines hard to see.

The interpretation of the hairline is determined by the gender of the person you are reading. A slightly receding hairline is considered fortunate in a man, as it reveals more of his forehead. In a woman, this is considered unfortunate, as it indicates problems in intimate relationships. A woman's hair should reach down toward the eyebrows, but not cover them.

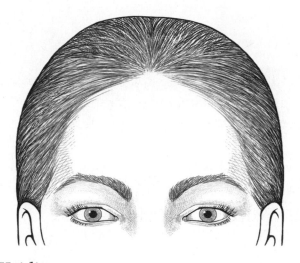

Narrow Hairline

A narrow hairline occurs when the hair on the forehead angles back to the temples, leaving a smaller than usual hairline above the forehead. People with narrow hairlines conform, and find it hard to disagree with others, or put their point of view forward.

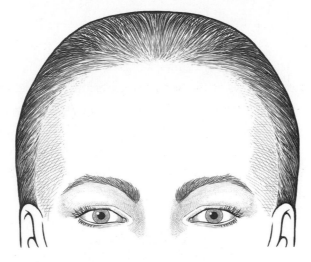

Wide Hairline

People with wide hairlines don't mind standing up for themselves. They ask questions, and then make up their own minds on the course of action they'll take. Usually, they were rebellious in the teenage years.

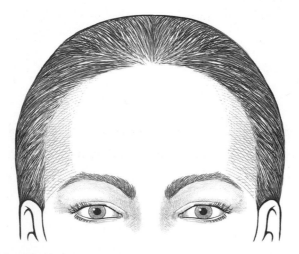

Smooth Hairline

A smooth hairline can be straight or curved. It appears to be mani-cured, as the hairline is smooth and has no irregularities. People with smooth hairlines are gracious, sociable, and easy to get on with.

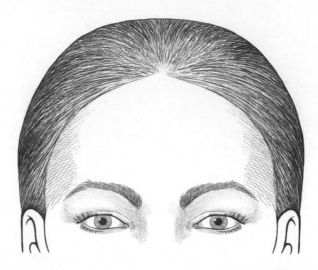

Curved Hairline

People with curved hairlines are reliable, reasonable, charming, and conscientious. They have a strong desire to do well financially.

Straight Hairline

It is rare to find a woman with a straight hairline, but it's found frequently in men. People with straight headlines are loyal, hard-working, thrifty, family-minded, and cautious. They need frequent encouragement, and become dispirited when their hard work is not given its due recognition.

M-Shaped Hairline

This type of hairline is also found mainly on men. People with M-shaped hairlines are strong, devoted, creative, considerate, and loving. They are said to be excellent lovers. John Wayne and Marlon Brando are two film stars who had this type of hairline.

Widow's Peak

Most people are familiar with the widow's peak, which is an extreme form of the M-shaped hairline. This occurs when the hairline comes to a distinct point in the center of the forehead. The V-shape that this creates is called the widow's peak. This came about because the hairline reminded people of the peak of a widow's hood, and made them think the person might die prematurely.

People with a widow's peak possess excellent creative imaginations, and this helps them come up with unique solutions to problems. They are frequently charismatic, too. Andy Garcia, Keanu Reeves, John Travolta, and Steven Seagal are good examples of people with a widow's peak. Marilyn Monroe also had a widow's peak. Eddie Munster, a character in the popular TV show *The Munsters*, had an extremely well-pronounced widow's peak.

Receding Hairline

Although many men fear becoming bald, in Chinese face reading a receding hairline is considered highly positive. If someone becomes bald after the age of fifty, it's considered a sign of superior intelligence.

A bald head is considered lucky in China, and can be a sign of financial success. The three great Sages of China—Confucius, Lao Tze, and Mencius—were all bald. Buddha was almost bald. Shou Xing, the Chinese God of Longevity, has a bald head and carries a peach, which is the Chinese symbol of longevity. He is also one of the three gods of happiness. Shou Xing, popularly known as Shou-Lao, decides on the time of each person's death.

It's highly auspicious if the balding starts at the forehead and the hairline gradually recedes. It's not considered a positive sign if the balding starts in the middle or back of the head.

It's a sign of open-mindedness and a quick brain if the balding starts from both sides of the forehead, leaving a goodly amount of hair in the center.

Hair in the Ears

Interestingly, in China, it was considered a good sign if hair sprouted from the ears. This is because it shows the person has a good brain and is likely to live a long life. However, these people frequently fail to make the most of their opportunities, as they spend too much time on frivolous, unimportant activities.

Beards

Beards were traditionally considered a sign of passion and virility, especially if the beard was long and lustrous. If the beard was thick, the person would be energetic, capable, efficient, and loving. If the beard felt stiff, the person would have problems making and keeping money. A long white beard was said to make old age more pleasant, and helped the person remain mentally young.

In China, it was believed that if someone grew a mustache and a long beard he could turn bad luck into good luck. However, if he grew a beard, but neglected to grow a mustache, his bad luck would worsen.

People grow beards for many reasons. It might be to appear more masculine, or because they simply like it. They may grow a beard to conceal a weak chin, a double chin, or some other perceived imperfection. Some people want to change their appearance, or appear intellectual or artistic. It might be a fashion statement. They might want to look older or more distinguished. Many young men grow a beard for fun. Some of them like it, and decide to keep it. Some people grow a beard because they dislike shaving. In some parts of the world people grow beards to help keep them warm in winter. Some people grow beards for religious reasons.

Nowadays, beards are not considered such an important symbol of masculinity, strength, and wisdom, and most men live an entire lifetime without growing one. This may well be fortunate, as many people with beards want to control and organize others.

In the next chapter we'll examine the significance of moles in the art of face reading.

I always hated my mole growing up. I even thought about having
it removed. At the time I didn't do it because I thought it would hurt,
and now I'm glad I didn't.
—NIKI TAYLOR

chapter 10

MOLES

Maculomancy, which means divination from the size, shape, and placement of birthmarks, originated in China as part of physiognomy. Hippocrates (c.460–c.377 BCE), the traditional father of medicine, was particularly interested in the subject.[1]

In Chinese face reading moles are considered highly auspicious, as most of the time they provide good luck, and enhance the potential of the part of the face they are found on. Moles need to be raised from the skin to be read.

The most fortunate moles are round, as they enhance the person's good luck. Oblong moles enhance the person's wealth. Moles that are dark in color are more propitious than lighter-colored moles.

A mole on the chin provides determination, tenacity, and stubbornness. These people succeed through sheer will power and an inability to give up. If they achieve wealth, and they frequently do, they gain pleasure from being generous with their fortune. They are also highly intuitive. Mao Tse Tung (1893–1976), formerly Chairman of the People's Republic of China, had a large mole on the left side of his chin.

A mole close to the mouth provides additional energy that is used to enhance the person's ability to enjoy the pleasures of life. It also enhances the person's sympathy and support for the less fortunate people in his or her local community. Supermodel Cindy Crawford has a mole immediately to the left of her mouth.

A mole on either cheek denotes someone who is generous, sympathetic, kind-hearted, and easy to get on with. These people enjoy light-hearted flirting, and remain young at heart, all the way through life.

A mole on the nose, or close to it, shows the person will experience difficulties in achieving his or her goals. This applies especially to the person's career.

A mole close to an eye provides the person with confidence, a serious approach to life, and the ability to disregard the frivolous and focus on what is really important. Actor Ben Affleck has a mole close to his left eye.

A mole on an eyelid is considered inauspicious, as people with it experience more than their fair share of ups and downs as they go through life.

A mole in, or beside, an eyebrow provides the person with courage, and the ability to stand up for what he or she considers to be right. Tiger Woods has a mole in this position.

A mole on the upper half of an ear is a sign of good luck and financial security. If the mole is on the lower half of the ear, the person will enjoy full use of his or her mental faculties throughout a long life.

A mole on the forehead enhances the person's career, as it provides focus, drive, and energy. However, it's not considered nearly as fortunate in love and romance, as it shows the person might neglect this side of life because he or she is so focused on career success.

Moles that are hidden—perhaps in the eyebrows, beard, or hair—are considered extremely fortunate. In fact, hidden moles are much luckier than moles that are visible. This is because they show the person has all the qualities necessary for success. These literally mean a fortunate life.

Moleosophy, the study of moles, plays a role in Vedic astrology.[2] In India, moles on the right side of the body are considered auspicious for men, while moles on the left side are considered auspicious for women.

A mole in the center of the forehead indicates the person will make money, but have a bad temper.

A mole on the right side of the forehead indicates wealth after the age of thirty.

A mole on the left side of the forehead is a sign of worry over financial matters.

A mole on the right eyebrow indicates travel, wealth, and a successful business.

A mole on the left eyebrow indicates foolish decisions, and bad luck in business.

A mole on an ear is a sign of good luck. If the person has a mole on each ear, he or she will be influential, and enjoy a comfortable and successful life.

A mole on the tip of the nose is a sign of good luck, and fast progress.

A mole on the right side of the nose shows the person will travel a great deal.

A mole on the left side of the nose indicates considerable success with the opposite sex. However, this person needs to be careful, as he or she is prone to accidents.

A mole on the upper lip indicates the person will be charismatic, charming, and persuasive, especially with the opposite sex.

A mole on the lower lip shows the person will be studious and conscientious.

Moles on the cheeks are always propitious, and denote success as long as the person sets goals and is prepared to work hard to achieve them.

A mole on the center of the chin indicates someone who is fair, kind, generous, and ultimately wealthy.

A mole on the left side of the chin indicates someone who is studious, and interested in spiritual growth.

A mole on the right side of the chin indicates slow, but steady, progress. People with this achieve status and a good reputation.

If you have moles anywhere on your body, you should have them checked regularly to make sure they don't change color, size, or shape. Even if they're in a highly auspicious position, you shouldn't hesitate to have them removed if your doctor feels it's necessary.

Many people want to know if face readers interpret freckles. Freckles don't have a specific meaning in physiognomy, but are considered to be a sign of playfulness and friendliness. This agrees with the old saying: "The more freckles a person has, the more friends he or she will have." An Irish friend of mine, who is well adorned with freckles, told me an Irish saying on the subject: "A face without freckles is like a night without stars."

In the next chapter we'll give two people a brief reading based on everything we've learned so far.

A beautiful face is a silent commendation.
—FRANCIS BACON

chapter 11

PUTTING IT TOGETHER

Most of the time, people have no idea that I'm reading their faces. I use the information I gain from observing faces to help me communicate better with the people I interact with in the course of my life. It's useful to know at a glance if someone is an optimist or a pessimist, is outgoing or reserved, or prefers an overview of the situation, rather than all the details.

Every now and again, I get asked to read someone's face. This gives me a wonderful opportunity to examine someone's face in depth, and see all the various aspects of his or her personality clearly revealed for anyone with the interest or time to look.

I have also done face reading professionally as entertainment at corporate events. These readings are extremely popular, and there's always a long line of people waiting for their turn. Because the readings have to be done quickly, there's time to point out only the most obvious features, rather than provide an in-depth reading.

No matter what type of face reading you do, there are a number of things you need to keep in mind.

1. You must never give a face reading to anyone without his or her permission.

2. Be kind and gentle. People are extremely sensitive and, as you're dealing with people's feelings, you must be careful and tactful.

3. You must focus on people's positive attributes, unless you're asked about a particular problem or concern.

4. You cannot discuss anything you see in someone's face with others. Face reading is confidential.

5. You are bound to see qualities you don't like in some people's faces. If you discuss these, you must do so in an impartial, non-judgmental way.

6. You must be open-minded.

7. Remember you're not infallible. Consequently, you're bound to make mistakes from time to time.

A good way to practice face reading is to build up a collection of photographs that you can examine at your leisure. However, this has one major disadvantage. Photographs can't give you the feedback that real people can. It's a good idea to start with photographs, and once you've become used to the process, start reading for people. Most people are flattered if you tell them they have an interesting face, and would they mind if you read it. Tell them you're a beginner, and are grateful for the opportunity to practice. Once people know you're studying the subject, your popularity will increase, as most people are intrigued with the subject and would love to have a face reading.

When I read people's faces I start by looking for an outstanding characteristic, such as a large nose, thin lips, or forward facing ears. I continue by studying the face in a set order:

1. Look for any outstanding characteristics. Examples include a large nose, high- or low-set ears, moles, an extremely large mouth, or virtual absence of the philtrum.

2. Determine the shape of the face.

3. Look at the forehead. Is it broad or narrow?

4. Look at the ears from the front and the side. Are they large or small? Are they set high or low?

5. Look at the eyebrows and eyes. Are the eyebrows low or high? What shape are they? Do they curve, run in a straight line, or head up or down? Are the eyes large or small?

6. Look at the nose. Is it large, small, or medium? What shape is it? Are the nostrils large or small? What shape is the tip?

7. Look at the mouth. Do the ends curve up or down? Are the lips thin or full? Is one lip larger than the other?

8. Look at the philtrum. Is it long or short? Is it wider at one end than the other?

9. Look at the cheeks. Are the cheekbones prominent? Are the cheeks plump and rounded? Flat or full? What lines are visible?

10. Look at the chin. Is it long or short? Narrow or broad?

11. Now it's time to examine the person's profile. See what the forehead, nose, and chin look like from the side. Look at the lips, also, to determine if one of the person's lips protrude.

12. Check the back of the head. Is the shape round, square, or egg-shaped? Is the head broad or narrow?

13. Look at the person's hair, and determine if it is thick or thin, curly or straight. Check the hairline.

14. Once you have mentally checked all of this, you can start your reading.

Sample Reading

Let's assume you're reading the face of an attractive woman in her early thirties. She has:

Oval face

Large ambition zone

Rounded forehead with three horizontal lines

Small round ears that hug the head, rounded helix, small earlobes

Eyebrows thin, high set, and long

Large, sparkling blue eyes with rounded corners

Large straight nose, with a downward tip; small nostrils

Large mouth, full lips (top lip fuller than bottom lip; upturned corners
  to the mouth

Long, deep philtrum; straight philtrum

Curved cheeks

Round chin

Head shape round and narrow

Long hair; curved hairline

With this information, you might tell her:

"[Oval face] You have a fascinating face, from a face reading point of view. Your face is oval, and this shows that you're a caring person who gets on well with others. You're a logical thinker, and use your unique perspective to look at problems from a number of different viewpoints. However, you also change your mind frequently, so people don't always know what you really think. You use logic well, but you're also highly intuitive, and you've found this extremely useful in your everyday dealings with others. You have many interests, but you're better at starting them, and sometimes find it hard to finish them. I think your brain is so quick that you often lose interest.

"[Ambition zone] You keep your feet firmly on the ground, and because you enjoy the rewards of success, you're prepared to work hard and long to achieve it. You're poised, and have an air of refinement about you that is recognized by others. You never settle for second best.

"[Forehead] You have a rounded forehead, and this increases your imagination. There are several factors on your face that reveal your excellent imagination. You should always seek out work that is mentally stimulating and satisfying. You get bored easily, and tend to float away into your imagination much of the time. [Three horizontal lines] You have three creases on your forehead. This shows you have a good memory, and can be something of a worrier.

"[Rounded ears] Your ears are rounded, and this makes you sociable and outgoing. A large number of creative people have rounded ears. [Small ears] The size of your ears tells me you're thoughtful, careful, cautious, and ambitious. You may not let on to others how ambitious you actually are, but the energy is there, and you should aim high. [Ears flat against the head] You are tactful, forgiving, sensitive, and a good listener. [Rounded helix] The outer rim of your ear is well formed and rounded. This tells me that you need plenty of mental stimulation. You have a great deal of physical energy, as well, and you enjoy having a good time. [Conch less prominent than the helix] Although you have all the abilities necessary for success, you'll need to push yourself to achieve your goals. [Earlobes] Your earlobes tell me that you live very much in the present, rather than dwelling on the past, or daydreaming about the future. They also tell me that patience is not one of your strong points.

"[Eyebrows] Your eyebrows are long and thin. This shows that you sometimes tend to get bogged down in all the details. Most of the time, you'd rather hear a summary than listen to every single point. [Long eyebrows] You get on well with your family and friends. I think you came from a secure home and had a good upbringing in a loving family. You make a special effort to remain in contact with close friends and family. You have good taste, and like having nice things around you. [High set] You're fun loving and easy to get along with. However, you can also be aloof and detached at times.

"[Eyes] I'm sure you know the expression, 'eyes are the windows to the soul.' You have beautiful eyes. [Large eyes] They tell me that you're friendly and able to express your feelings easily. You're intelligent and have a good imagination. [Sparkling eyes] You have bright eyes that reflect your passion for life. You are enthusiastic and need to be busy. [Rounded corners] The nicely rounded corners of your eyes show that you're loyal, and devoted to the people you care about. You're also extremely kind.

"[Nose] You possibly didn't like your nose when you were younger, but from a face reading point of view, you have a wonderful nose. Your nose tells me you enjoy life to the full, and make the most of every opportunity that comes your way. [Long nose] Long noses have always been considered aristocratic, so you may have connections to royalty somewhere way back in your family tree. A long nose shows that you're conscientious, responsible, and speak your mind when you feel it's necessary. You have a strong sense of right and wrong. The downside of having a long nose is that you're inclined to be stubborn. [Down-turned tip] The tip of your nose turns downward, showing that you can judge a person, or assess a situation, at a glance. It's a useful trait. You're also shrewd when it comes to money matters. I think you're careful with your money, and look after it well. [Small nostrils] Your nostrils also tell me you're careful in money matters. I doubt if you spend your money flippantly or on the spur of the moment.

"[Mouth] You have a large mouth, with full lips. [Large mouth] This shows that you're generous, understanding, and forgiving. You have a great time with the people you love, and enjoy a good, healthy, physical relationship with the one special person in your life. [Full lips] You're friendly, sociable, affectionate, and sensual. [Top lip fuller than bottom] Although both of your lips are full, the upper lip is fuller than the bottom one. This tells me that you're a good conversationalist, and can talk freely about virtually anything. [Upturned corners] You're an optimist, and have a positive approach to everything you do. You have a good sense of fun, and enjoy making people laugh. [Long, deep philtrum] The groove that connects your nose and mouth is called the philtrum. Yours is long, and well defined. This shows that you're happiest inside a good, close, stable relationship, ideally with a family. If you don't have children, the nurturing quality your philtrum provides will be used elsewhere, probably in some form of creativity. [Straight philtrum] The two lines marking your philtrum are parallel. This shows you're a good administrator. It also means you'll manage to balance your home and working lives, and be successful in both.

"[Curved cheeks] You have beautiful, rounded cheeks. These show that although you get along well with virtually everyone, you still need quiet times on your own. Some people want others around them all the time, but you need time to contemplate and ponder what's going on in your life. I think you make better decisions as a result of this. [Cheek lines] You have well-marked lines running from your nose down either side of your mouth. This shows that you've learned from experience, as well as from all the hard work you've had to put in to get where you are now. You have faint lines that curve below your eyes. These show that you set goals sometimes, but at other times you're happy to simply take life as it comes.

"[Chin] You have a round chin, and this makes you sympathetic and supportive. You enjoy helping others. You may deliberately hold yourself back at times, especially if others are trying to put you into a leadership role.

"Now we'll look at the back of your head. [Head shape] Your head forms a gentle curve at the top of your head. This shows that you're confident in your ability to do the things you want to do. You get along well with others, and stand up for yourself when necessary. [Narrow head] You have a great deal of self-control. You tend to worry about what other people think, and this sometimes holds you back.

"[Hair] You wear your hair long, and this shows that you're practical, level-headed, and keep your feet on the ground. You enjoy coming up with new ideas, and discussing them with others. [Curved hairline] Your hairline has a gentle curve to it. This shows that you're charming, efficient, conscientious, and practical. You're prepared to work hard to achieve your goals.

"There are few contradictions in your face, and it looks as if your life is progressing pretty much as it should be. Your positive approach to everything you do will stand you in good stead in the future. You have a wonderful face."

Sample Reading Two

Let's assume you're reading the face of a businessman in his middle forties. He has:

Square face

Large practical zone

Broad forehead; two horizontal lines, and two frown lines

Large, forward facing, squarish ears, with large lobes; high set

Long, thick, curved, low-set eyebrows

Small, wide-set eyes, with upward curving corners; curved upper eyelids

Large, Roman nose with wide tip and small nostrils

Mole on side of nose

Medium-sized mouth, with narrow lips; upturned mouth.

Well marked, short philtrum; philtrum is wider at the bottom

Fleshy cheeks, two main cheek lines

Broad chin

Square, broad head

Short hair, receding hairline

For this person you might say:

"[Square face] You are a practical, down-to-earth sort of person. I think you could turn your hand to almost anything that interests you. You are persistent, patient, and have the ability to motivate and inspire others. You have the ability to show other people how to do things that you can do. Once they know how to do it, you're happy to step aside, as you're confident they'll do the job properly. You are ambitious, and you're well on the way to achieving your goals.

"[Large practical zone] You have a strong, almost sensual, approach to life. You have strong physical appetites. You keep your feet firmly on the ground. You're basically a logical person, but you're aware of your gut feelings, and have learned to act on them, too. In fact, you're relying on them more and more, as time goes on.

"[Broad forehead] Your forehead indicates a wide range of interests. There's a possible contradiction here, as your forehead indicates a dislike for details. Your eyebrows say the opposite. I think this is probably because you often try to do too much, and don't have enough time to finish everything you try to do. Interestingly, you'll always pick up new interests as you go through life. This helps keep you forever young. Your forehead also shows that you work best in a position of authority, as you possess considerable business and management acumen. [Two horizontal lines] The two main lines crossing your forehead are long and deep. This is a sign of popularity, and gives you a natural ability to get on well with others. [Two frown lines] The two frown lines relate to your family and loved ones. They show that you work hard to make sure everyone is noticed, loved, appreciated, and cared for. You don't play favorites. Everyone in the family is showered with the same amount of love and attention.

"[Large ears] Your ears are good-sized. In Chinese face reading, this is a sign of both longevity and good luck. [Large earlobes] This is especially the case if the person has good ear lobes, as you do. [Squarish tops and sides] You are shrewd, and able to see the essentials of a situation at a glance. You're also capable of tackling a number of tasks at the same time. [Forward facing ears] Your ears are fairly prominent, and you might have been teased a bit about them when you were a child. However, from a face reading point of view, you have excellent ears. They show that you're independent, and don't like being told what to do. You like to make your own mind up on important decisions that concern you. These ears also make you stubborn. The other advantage of your type of ear is that you tend to attract money. [High-set ears] The placement of your ears emphasizes qualities I've already mentioned: you're reliable, conscientious, down-to-earth, and ambitious. [Helix and conch well defined] The two main visible parts of your ear—the outer and inner circles—are both equally well defined. This shows that you have the necessary motivation, ability, and tenacity to achieve whatever degree of success you aspire to.

"[Eyebrows] You have long, thick, gently curved eyebrows. All of these qualities are good. [Thick eyebrows] You like to know the whole story, and enjoy the details just as much as the overall picture. [Long eyebrows] Your long eyebrows show that you get along well with your family and friends. You probably enjoyed a happy childhood, and want your family to be just as happy. When it comes to family, you're generous with your time, as well as money. You're prepared to stand up for what you think is right. [Low-set] The placement of your eyebrows shows that you're open, friendly, and enjoy helping others. You can be impatient at times, too.

"[Small eyes] Your eyes tell me that you find it hard to express your innermost feelings. You tend to keep your emotions firmly in check most of the time. [Wide-set eyes] You have the ability to see an entire situation at a glance. You have a retentive memory, and can remember things from way back in your early childhood. You'll always appear younger than your years. You'll also always be broad-minded, and have many interests. Because of all your different activities, you probably have difficulty in finishing everything you start. [Upward curving corners] You may have noticed that the outer edges of your eyes curve upward. This shows you're reliable, faithful, and have a good sense of humor. [Curved upper eyelids] Your upper eyelids have a nice curve to them, and this makes you forever young at heart. You always need something ahead to look forward to. Your curved upper eyelids also mean you enjoy helping others.

"[Large, Roman nose] You have a striking nose, and this gives you energy and personal power. It shows you like to be in charge, ideally in a position of considerable responsibility. You handle your own personal finances well, and are inclined to play your financial cards close to your chest. [Wide tip] The tip of your nose is wide, and this shows that you're tolerant, diplomatic, and tactful. Of course, you're critical at times, but by and large, you take people as you find them. [Small nostrils] You're careful with your money, and don't spend frivolously. You like to investigate serious purchases carefully first to make sure that you actually need it. [Mole on side of nose] You have a mole on the side of your nose. Moles are always interpreted in face reading. A mole in this position shows that you'll sometimes feel you're working twice as hard as other people to get where you want to go. It's a sign of success, but only after a great deal of hard work and effort.

"[Mouth] Your mouth is about average in size. This shows that you're tolerant, understanding, honest, and able to fit in to most situations. [Thin lips] Your lips tell me that you're determined, persistent, and decisive. You keep your thoughts and feelings well under control. Interestingly, many politicians have similar lips to you. You've never liked being teased. This probably dates back to your school days. [Upturned mouth] You're cheerful, positive, and optimistic 99.9 percent of the time. [Short philtrum] The groove that joins your nose and lips reveals the same thing that your lips did: you don't enjoy being teased. [Well-marked philtrum] Fortunately, this groove also shows you have almost limitless reserves of energy, and have the potential to be highly creative. [Philtrum wider at the bottom] The proper name for this groove is the philtrum. Your philtrum widens as it heads toward your mouth. This shows that you'll learn all the way through life. It also shows that you'll gain knowledge, wisdom, and wealth as you mature. This sometimes also indicates a later than usual marriage, or permanent relationship.

"[Fleshy cheeks] Your cheeks tell me that you're a happy person, someone who makes the most of every situation, and enjoys sampling pretty well everything life has to offer. You are spontaneous, and can surprise others, even people who've known you for a long time.

[Cheek lines] You have two strong lines running from the side of your nose to the sides of your mouth. These reveal the hard work you've put in to become the person you are today. They also show that you'll continue working hard to achieve your goals.

"[Broad chin] Your chin reveals your ambition. It also shows that you're confident of your own abilities, and always do things with a definite purpose in mind. However, it also shows the difficulty you have in expressing your innermost feelings. Your eyes give the same message, so this is an area you should work on.

"[Back of the head] Now we'll have a quick look at the back of your head. [Square] This shows that you're reliable and cautious. You think carefully before making a decision, but once you've made it, you follow through with great determination. [Broad head] The width of your head tells me that you have plenty of drive and ambition. You're better at giving orders than you are at receiving them. You can be demanding and controlling, if you think the situation requires it.

"[Short hair] You keep your hair short. This shows that you're decisive, energetic, and goal-oriented. You may well be interested in watching or playing a sport. [Receding hairline] Although men usually hate losing their hair, it's considered highly auspicious in Chinese face reading, as it's a sign of high intelligence, good luck, and financial success. Your hair is starting to recede, so you'll shortly become aware of the face reading benefits of this.

"You have a strong face, full of character. It looks as if you're in the right field for you, and you're making good, steady progress. Your family will always be the prime focus of your life, and no matter how old you ultimately become, you'll remain extremely close to your wife and children."

In the next chapter we'll start looking at facial expressions, one of the most important aspects of nonverbal communication.

Part Two
HOW TO READ
FACIAL EXPRESSIONS

The expression a woman wears on her face is far more important
than the clothes she wears on her back.

—DALE CARNEGIE

chapter 12

YOUR EXPRESSIONS SPEAK LOUDER THAN YOU

Sigmund Freud (1856–1939), founder of the psychoanalytic school of psychology, was well aware of the power of body language and facial expressions. He wrote: "He who has eyes to see and ears to hear may convince himself that no mortal can keep a secret. If his lips are silent, he chatters with his fingertips; betrayal oozes out of him at every pore."[1]

When Honoré de Balzac (1799–1850), the French novelist, visited Vienna for the first time, he couldn't speak the language or understand the currency. He was concerned that cab drivers would take advantage of this and came up with a simple strategy based on the drivers' faces. When he arrived at his destination, he'd give the driver a single coin. If the driver's hand remained held open, he'd add another coin. He'd continue placing one coin at a time onto the driver's palm until the driver smiled. At that point, Balzac would take back the last coin and leave, happy that he had paid enough, but not too much.[2]

There are said to be six facial emotions that are found all around the world. They are easy to recognize: surprise, happiness, fear, anger, disgust, and sadness. Because these emotions can be read so easily, people tend to mask or hide them in situations when they don't want their true feelings known.

In the 1960s, Albert Mehrabian, a psychologist and expert on nonverbal communication, came to the conclusion that there were three elements in face-to-face encounters: the words, tone of voice, and body language. He found that words made up a mere seven percent of the impression given, while the tone of voice accounted for 38 percent, and body language 55 percent. This is sometimes called the "3 Vs": Verbal, Vocal, and Visual. The body language component was 15 percent for appearance, and 40 percent for facial expressions and movements. However, his experiments involved people's feelings and attitudes, which means these percentages may not be correct in other situations. All the same, they reveal how important the face is in all person-to-person communications.[3]

It is important to recognize and interpret people's non-spoken facial communication. Not only will it make your path through life that much easier and more enjoyable, but it will also ensure you enjoy greater success in every area of your life.[4] It's a fascinating skill to develop, and one you already know a great deal about. For instance, you can probably tell at a glance if a friend is angry, anxious, bored, contented, frustrated, interested, stressed, or tired. If you can read these on a friend, the chances are you can also read them on the face of a stranger.

Have you ever gritted your teeth, stiffened your upper lip, trembled with rage, or blushed with embarrassment? Because you've experienced these yourself, whenever you see these facial expressions in others, you'll instantly know what they mean.

We all subconsciously pick up the nonverbal traits of the society we live in. However, our personalities dictate how we utilize them.

Our thoughts, especially our emotions, dictate how we nonverbally express ourselves to others.

There are localized variations, but most nonverbal cues are universal. I travel a great deal, and find my knowledge of nonverbal communication helps me explain what I need when I can't speak the language. This makes my travel smoother and more enjoyable.

Imagine walking into your favorite coffee shop and seeing someone you know. How would you feel if the person smiled, and at the same time, raised his or her eyebrows?

Imagine walking into the same coffee shop and seeing someone else you know. How would you feel if the person smiled, and at the same time squinted for a brief moment?

The person who raised his or her eyebrows momentarily likes you, but the person who squinted doesn't, even though he or she smiled.

The person who smiled and squinted provided an example of a facial disconnect. These occur when the person's facial expression doesn't agree with what he or she is saying. If you happen to come across someone you don't like at a party, you might chat with him or her for a minute or two. Although you'd both be smiling, and talking in an apparently friendly manner, someone watching your facial expressions and body language would be able to tell you didn't like each other.

It has been estimated that people can make more than ten thousand different nonverbal facial expressions. Fortunately, we don't need to interpret them all.

Facial expressions are complicated by the fact that from an early age we're taught to put on a false face. When I was very young, I remember my mother telling me to smile when certain relatives came to visit. She was effectively telling me to lie with my face. We are all good at this. We've learned how to control our facial expressions, in the hope of disguising our true feelings.

Some unfortunate people have lost the ability to make involuntary facial expressions. Some stroke victims suffer from paralysis of one side of the face. People who suffer from Parkinson's disease have a limited range of involuntary facial expressions, though, oddly, they can voluntarily make them if they wish.[5] Unfortunately, most people see their inability to make appropriate involuntary facial expressions as a lack of interest, and this compounds their problems. My wife and I have an acquaintance who has become a semi-recluse as his Parkinson's disease slowly worsens. He told me that people speak to his wife, but virtually ignore him, as they feel he isn't interested in what they have to say. It's sad that this intelligent, erudite man is withdrawing from society because people fail to appreciate his problem.

Some people are experts at concealing their emotions. There are times when it makes sense to do this. You may not want to look elated at receiving a pay raise while sitting with colleagues who didn't. You certainly don't want to show your true feelings when receiving a good hand at poker. You might want to conceal your feelings after receiving bad news over the phone. However, even feelings such as these can be read by others, as it's impossible to totally conceal all our feelings.

Actors are able to manipulate their facial expressions when on stage or in front of a camera. Unfortunately, so do other people who try to fool us with false tears and fake smiles. Con men and women are the perfect example.

Some years ago, I was about to enter a library in Los Angeles when an attractively dressed woman approached me and told me that she had an urgent appointment in Pasadena, but someone had stolen her car, which also contained her purse and credit cards. She needed forty dollars for cab fare. She promised to return it to me as soon as she returned home. This lady was extremely convincing, and if I hadn't been watching the local news a couple of nights earlier, I would have fallen for her story. A segment of the news warned people to beware of well-dressed women claiming their cars had broken down and they needed money for a cab fare. This woman was performing this exact confidence trick. She had no appointment in Pasadena, and I'm sure her car was parked just around the corner. Because I knew exactly what she was doing, thanks to the TV news, I paid especial attention to everything she said and did. Her body language, and facial expressions were perfect. She should have been an actress.

Because people can use their expressions to deceive others, you need to look at a series of facial cues, known as clusters, to discover what someone is really feeling.

The Universal Expressions

We've already mentioned the six universal expressions that everyone around the world knows: surprise, happiness, fear, anger, disgust, and sadness. Here are the usual actions that accompany these feelings.

Surprise

Surprise is revealed by the forehead, eyebrows, eyes, and mouth. The eyebrows rise and curve, the horizontal lines on the forehead crease, the whites of the eyes become visible, and the jaw drops open.

Happiness

Happiness is usually expressed as a warm smile. It is revealed by the eyes, mouth, and cheeks. The lower eyelids rise slightly, and wrinkles appear beneath them. The eyes sparkle, and crow's feet may appear at the corners of the eyes. The mouth stretches outward and upward, emphasizing the lines that run from the side of the nose to outside the corners of the mouth. These lines force the cheeks to rise and swell outward. Usually, the mouth will open slightly to expose the upper teeth.

Fear

Fear is revealed by the eyebrows, forehead, eyes, and mouth. The eyebrows rise and are pulled together. The lines in the forehead become more visible, and are partially creased in the center of the forehead.

The eyelids rise, exposing the whites of the eyes. The lips are pulled sideways in a horizontal line. Sometimes the lips part slightly.

Anger

Anger is revealed by the eyebrows, eyes, mouth, and sometimes the nose. The eyebrows are drawn down and inward, emphasizing the frown lines. The upper and lower eyelids close slightly to narrow the eyes, which stare coldly at whatever caused the anger. The lips are compressed, and turned down slightly at the corners. Some people also flare their nostrils.

Disgust

Disgust is revealed by the eyes, nose, mouth, and cheeks. The lower eyelids rise, creating fine horizontal lines in the skin immediately below the eyes. The nose wrinkles, and this causes the cheeks to rise. The upper lip curls and rises in the center.

Sadness

Sadness is revealed by the mouth, eyebrows, and forehead. The mouth is slack, and droops at each corner. Sometimes the lips quiver. The inner ends of the eyebrows rise, emphasizing the frown lines and the center of the horizontal lines on the forehead. Frequently, the eyes are crying, or appear to be on the brink of shedding tears.

The Face from the Top of the Head to the Neck

Hair

People who touch, stroke, or fondle their hair are subconsciously seeking reassurance. This dates back to early childhood memories of a parent, or some other loved one, stroking their head to provide comfort and love.

People who twist their hair are suffering from anxiety or stress. Although the stress may be in the distant past, the hair twisting often continues, as it becomes a habit.

People who are harassed or stressed often run their fingers through their hair to provide temporary relief.

Women sometimes stroke, ruffle, rearrange, or run their fingers through their hair to show off its length and beauty when in the company of someone they find attractive. This is usually, but not necessarily, done subconsciously.

The Head Nod

In most parts of the world it's a sign of assent when someone nods his or her head. Consequently, nodding the head usually means yes. (However, in Bulgaria, Turkey, Serbia, Montenegro, Slovenia, Iran, and parts of Greece, nodding the head up and down signifies no. They shake their heads from side to side to indicate yes.[6])

Head nods are also used in conversations. People nod their heads when listening to someone talking to them. This serves two purposes: it tells the speaker that they're listening to what he or she is saying, and it also tells the speaker that they're happy to keep on listening, at least for the moment.

Nodding rapidly shows that the person is aware of the urgency of the situation, or wants to speak.

A slow, prolonged nod is a sign that the person doesn't fully agree with what has been said.

Most of the time, if someone wants the speaker to stop talking, all he or she needs to do is stop nodding. This tells the speaker that the person has heard enough. When the speaker stops, the person can have his or her say, or end the conversation.

The Head Shake

Shaking the head is just as universal as the head nod. It means no. If you're trying to sell something to someone, and he or she shakes his head, it's a sign that you need to change tack, and continue the sales pitch from a different direction. This headshake will probably be slight, as it's usually a subconscious reaction to what's being said.

Sometimes someone will shake his or her head slightly while speaking positively and enthusiastically about something. Whenever this occurs, the head shaking gesture reveals the person's true feelings, no matter how positive or enthusiastic the words might be.

Head Tilting

If someone holds his or her head up while you are talking, it's a sign of mild, polite interest.

If this person tilts his or her head slightly to one side while you are talking, it's a sign that they're listening and absorbing what you are saying. The tilt is often accompanied by occasional nods to encourage the speaker to continue.

Tilting the head to one side can also be a submissive gesture. This is a larger tilt that exposes part of the neck, a vulnerable part of the body. It also makes the person look smaller than he or she is, and makes him or her appear innocent and guileless.

People who want to appear submissive subconsciously use this gesture. A subordinate might tilt his or her head while conversing with someone who is more senior, or more important. Tilting the head can also make the person more sexually attractive, and some people deliberately adopt it when conversing with someone they are sexually attracted to.

Tapping the Head

Tapping the temple or forehead with an index finger is a sign that the person doing the tapping thinks the other person is crazy, or has said something so ridiculous that even the idea of it is crazy.

Tapping the head can also be a deliberate insult, suggesting that the other person is incapable of normal thought processes.

Interestingly, tapping the head can sometimes mean the person doing the tapping thinks the other person is extremely intelligent.

Hitting the Head or Face

A common gesture used by people when they have done something stupid is to gently slap or hit themselves on their heads. The blow is normally made on the side of the face, the forehead, or the top of the head.

Stressed Face

When people are stressed, their faces tense, their eyebrows knit, and their foreheads appear lined and uneven. They may also find it hard to make good eye contact, with their eyes flickering to and from the person speaking, or gazing at an imaginary spot in the middle distance. Eyelid fluttering can also occur.

Frowning

A furrowed forehead cannot be interpreted in isolation, as it occurs when people are anxious, upset, sad, angry, or concentrating on a task. Someone running late, and searching for his or her gate at an airport is likely to be frowning, as is someone who has just been stopped for speeding on the freeway. However, the same person may also frown when adding up a column of numbers, or waiting for a lengthy meeting to end.

Eyebrows

It's a sign of skepticism if one eyebrow is raised. Both eyebrows raised, especially if accompanied by an open mouth, is a sign of surprise.

People automatically lower their eyebrows when faced with a perceived threat. Eyebrows tend to be lowered when people are annoyed or angry. Eyebrow lowering can also be used to dominate or intimidate others. People who do this usually tighten their mouths at the same time. I've met several people who deliberately do this.

Apparently, they feel that if they look angry, people will be anxious to please them.

However, if the eyebrows are dropped too low, it's a sign of weakness, timidity, and insecurity. People tend to take advantage of people who habitually exhibit lowered eyebrows.

The eyebrows also reveal if someone is interested in you. If you meet someone for the first time, you'll probably smile. If the other person also smiles, but at the same time raises his or her eyebrows momentarily, it's a sign that he or she is interested in meeting you. If the person smiles, but the eyebrows fail to "flash," it's a sign that the person couldn't care less if he or she met you or not.

Eyes

Marcus Tillius Cicero (106–43 BCE) said, *"Ut imago est animi voltus sic indices oculi"* (The face is a picture of the mind as the eyes are its interpreter). This is probably where the famous expression "Eyes are the window of the soul" came from. Over time, this has become a cliché. Clichés usually contain a grain of truth, though, and eyes are extremely revealing to anyone able to read the nonverbal signals they produce. Phrases such as "if looks could kill," "she has come-hither eyes," "look at those bedroom eyes," "what a hateful stare," or "he has dead eyes" have come about because of the numerous expressions that can be made with them. A friend of mine writes extremely successful romance novels. In her books, the eyes of the heroes burn with desire, and the heroines' eyes melt as a result.

Victor Hugo (1802–1885), the famous French novelist, was almost as famous in his lifetime for his numerous love affairs. He explained part of the secret of his success with women in his *Memoirs*: "When a woman is speaking with you, monsieur," he wrote, "listen to what she says with your eyes."

Recently, at a cocktail party, I saw a young lady whose eyes were sparkling with happiness. Her partner said something to her, and in an instant the eyes changed from happiness to surprise to hurt. Although she was several yards away from me, in a different group of people, her feelings were obvious to anyone watching. The eyes reveal much more than we think because it's almost impossible to hide the emotional responses revealed in them.

The fact that our pupils dilate when we're showing interest in something or someone is possibly the best-known example of this. Most people cannot control this consciously. Our pupils dilate when we like what we see, and constrict when we are displeased or dislike what we see. The only way to consciously dilate your eyes is to think of something in the past that made your eyes dilate.

When you're surprised, excited, or stimulated, your eyes widen and the pupils dilate. This enables your brain to receive as much information as possible. If the surprise is positive, the pupils will remain dilated. However, if the surprise is a negative one, the pupils will constrict in a fraction of a second, providing the brain with a clearly focused picture of what is going on. This enables the person to deal with the situation in an appropriate way.[7]

The lighting in a room affects pupil dilation. If the room is very bright, the pupils will contract as a result of the harsh light. Likewise, if the room is dark, the pupils will dilate to provide greater vision. Therefore, although dilated pupils show the person is interested in you, you also need to check the lighting in the room to see what affect it might have on the other person's eyes.

Young children are taught not to stare. There can't be too many children who haven't been told, "It's rude to stare." Consequently, we all learn to look at someone momentarily, and then, without changing our facial expression, allow our gaze to move on. In public places, the gaze is about one second long. This time is extended slightly in social situations, as people size each other up.

You can show interest or, alternatively, challenge someone by allowing your gaze to linger longer than what is acceptable in your area.

A blank stare is insulting, as it means you're looking right through someone as if he or she wasn't there. The hate stare is even worse, and is a deliberate attempt to intimidate someone the person is prejudiced against.

Eye contact reveals interest. If you met someone at a party who looked into your eyes longer than usual, you'd think the person was interested in you, and would probably find them attractive.

People who avoid eye contact may be painfully shy, or could be trying to hide something. They might, for instance, be trying to hide the fact that they're attracted to you. They might have a guilty secret, or could be ashamed about something. They might be nervous or feel intimidated by you. They might be reliving painful emotions while telling you about a tragic event. They may be avoiding eye contact because they've told a lie.

The amount of eye contact varies from culture to culture. People in Greece enjoy looking at others, and want other people to study them. In fact, they feel ignored if other people show no interest in them. In Sweden, people look at others less often than most people in Europe, but when they do look, they look longer. Arabs use a great deal of eye contact, both when talking and listening.[8] In Japan, a direct gaze or stare is considered rude, and direct eye contact between two people of different genders is unacceptable.[9]

Some people come from a culture where eye contact is considered rude. When I was a student, I worked briefly at an abattoir, which employed a large number of young men from the Pacific Islands. Whenever the supervisor rebuked them, they would stare at the floor and giggle. That was appropriate behavior where they came from, but it used to infuriate the supervisors, who were offended by the lack of eye contact, which was made even worse by the nervous giggling. If the supervisors had known that this was how people in the Pacific Islands responded in this type of situation, they would have saved themselves a large amount of unnecessary stress.

People who suffer from autism and Asperger's syndrome also avoid eye contact. People who are suffering from anxiety often do the same.

People who are shy often prefer to give a sideways glance, instead of direct eye contact. They frequently look downward while doing this. Princess Diana is a good example of someone who did this. Desmond Morris, the British zoologist, author, and painter, calls this action "bold shyness," because although the shy person is looking at the other person, he or she is not staring directly, and is in fact demonstrating humility by looking away.

Eye contact is important in everyday conversation. The listener maintains more eye contact than the speaker. It has been estimated that the speaker maintains eye contact between 40 and 60 percent of the time, while the listener maintains eye contact about 80 percent of the time.[10] When the speaker has finished, he or she will look at the listener to let him or her know it's time to respond.

Eye contact also provides feedback to the person who is speaking. When you are looking at the speaker, you are paying attention to what is being said. However, if your eyes start wandering, the speaker will think you're not interested in what he or she is saying.

Direct eye contact is a sign of honesty, sincerity, confidence, and open communication. If you look at someone for more than a few seconds, he or she will subconsciously know that you're interested in him or her. However, too much eye contact can be intimidating to some people. Too little eye contact makes people wonder about your honesty, strength, and confidence. Someone who shifts his or her gaze away too quickly is considered to have "shifty eyes."

If you like someone, you'll look at him or her frequently. If you dislike someone, you'll look at him or her as little as possible. Consequently, if someone looks at you frequently during a conversation, it's a sign that he or she likes you.

Someone who constantly looks over your shoulder, or looks at other people in the room, while you're talking, is insulting you, as he or she is looking for someone more important to talk to.

Surprise

When people are surprised they open their eyes wide and show the sclera, or white of the eye, above the iris. Their eyebrows rise, and their lips part slightly. The mouth is relaxed, and sometimes drops open.

Fear

People who are scared or afraid open their eyes wide, and raise their eyebrows, which are drawn toward each other. Their lower eyelids tense, and the lips draw back in a straight line. Blinking increases, and the pupils dilate. This is sometimes called "a deer frozen in the headlights" expression.

Anger

People who are annoyed or angry stare directly at the person who has caused them to become angry. The eyebrows lower and create a frown. Both the upper and lower eyelids tense, causing the eyes to narrow. The jaw tenses, and blinking reduces to make the angry gaze more intimidating.

Disbelief or Doubt

People who question what has just been said narrow their eyes, furrow their brow, and raise an eyebrow. This can be a sign of disbelief or doubt.

Twitching Eyes

Twitching eyes are caused by a muscle spasm, and are a sign of stress and strain. They sometimes occur briefly when people are put into a difficult situation, such as being asked to make an impromptu speech.

Sometimes they can last for months. When this occurs, it's a sign to slow down, relax, and de-stress. Once the problem, whatever it happens to be, ends, the twitch will cease.

Shifty Eyes

Some people shift their eyes from side to side when they are upset, disturbed, embarrassed, or being insincere. It is the insincerity aspect that causes this to be known as "shifty eyes."

Shifting the eyes from side to side while looking downward is a sign of fear, treachery, disloyalty, and selfishness. These people are cowards who will do whatever they feel necessary to save themselves.

Eye Blocking

Eye blocking is always negative. It occurs when the person squints, closes, or covers his or her eyes. This often indicates disdain and dislike, but also occurs when the person feels threatened, distressed, or upset. Liars sometimes block their eyes while telling a lie.

Recently, a man came to me for help with his gambling addiction. He had lost a large amount of money through gambling, but told me that he'd let it go, and was moving forward again. As he told me this, one hand briefly covered his eyes, telling me that he was still upset and hadn't yet accepted the loss of the money.

Eye Dipping

Submissive people often avert their eyes downward to avoid offending someone who is more dominant. This is a deliberate, rather than a subconscious, gesture.

Eye dipping is also common when passing a stranger in the street. When the two people are about eight feet apart, both will lower their eyes until they have passed each other. By doing this each person indicates that he or she is non-threatening. In friendly neighborhoods, people might dip their heads, and then raise them to smile and say "hello" as they pass each other.

Eyes Closing

Blocking the eyes with a hand, or rubbing the eyes, shows that the person doesn't like what he or she is being told. If the person briefly touches an eye during a conversation, it's a sign that he doesn't think much of what the other person is saying.

When someone is given bad news, his or her eyes will close briefly in an attempt to block out the information. Some people put a hand over each eye, or block both eyes with one hand, when given bad news. If the person is holding an object, such as a book, he or she may use this to block the eyes.

If the person keeps his eyes closed for a number of seconds, it's a sign that he or she is processing negative emotions.

Sometimes the eyes will be squeezed tightly shut. When the eyes are compressed in this sort of way, it's a sign that the person is trying to deny, or block out, bad news.

Various forms of eye blocking can be seen by watching the coach of any losing team. In extreme cases, they'll sit with their head in their hands, with the eyes completely blocked.

Looking Over the Top of One's Spectacles

It's a sign of dominance to look at someone over the top of your spectacles. This look is even more threatening if the head is slightly dipped at the same time as the person looks over his or her glasses.

When I was at school, one of my teachers would deliberately lower his spectacles on his nose, and look over them to speak down to a child who hadn't been paying attention. It was his signature gesture, and the students who wore glasses would mimic it in the playground to get a laugh. Although it was amusing to mock this gesture, it was not comfortable to be the pupil this teacher spoke to over his glasses.

Looking Upward

If someone looks upward frequently while listening to someone else, he or she is bored, or doesn't approve of the way the conversation is going.

Rolling the eyes can also be a sign of impatience. If someone repeats a story several times to the same audience, one of the listeners might roll his or her eyes upward, to silently say, "There he goes again."

Looking Downward

Looking downward is a well-known sign of shyness and lack of confidence. It can also indicate a guilty conscience.

Squinting

Squinting is a sign of dislike and distrust. People tend to squint when acknowledging someone they don't like. The squint may last for only a fraction of a second, but is obvious to anyone who knows how to read faces.

People also squint when they're feeling uncomfortable. They often lower their eyebrows as well, indicating a loss of confidence.

If someone squints when reading a contract, or any other formal document, it's a sign of doubt and uncertainty. A good salesperson should be alert to this, and be ready to explain exactly what the clause means.

Some people deliberately lower their eyebrows and squint to appear aggressive and to intimidate others.

Direct Gaze

Lovers, as well as mothers and babies, stare into each other's eyes regularly. It's a sign of love, trust, and devotion. However, someone who is threatening you will also use a direct gaze and glare into your eyes. In this case, the person is using a threatening stare to try to intimidate you. Because a direct gaze can indicate both love and hate, you need to look at other factors to determine what is going on.

In our culture, it's considered rude to stare. This is why we look away at times while talking to others. This also helps us formulate our thoughts without the distraction of the other person's face.

Throughout history, high-status people have been free to look anywhere. Lower-status people don't necessarily have that right. This is why people humble themselves by bowing their heads in the presence of royalty or someone of elevated status.

Sideways Glance

The sideways glance occurs when someone lowers his or her head, and then looks sideways at the person they are communicating with. It shows the person is shy, demure, and coy. Princess Diana used this facial expression frequently. Unfortunately, this expression sends conflicting messages. It involves a stare, which is a bold gesture, coupled with a lowered head that indicates submission, shyness, and a lack of confidence. Consequently, many people find this expression annoying, though others find it charming and appealing.

Blinking and Fluttering

People blink more when they feel nervous, anxious, concerned, stressed, or upset. The blinking won't return to normal until they feel relaxed. President Richard M. Nixon exhibited "furious blinking" during his resignation speech. Because of this, Joseph Tecce, professor of psychology at Boston College, and an expert in body language, calls excessive blinking in uncomfortable situations the "Nixon effect." [11]

Eyelid flutter is more important, as it shows the person is upset about something. Not long ago, I was with a group of people and someone made an offensive remark about people who were gay. I'm sure it was intended as a joke rather than as a deliberate attempt to offend. Although the lady standing next to me didn't say anything, her eyelids began fluttering. As I was the host and wanted all my guests to feel comfortable, I immediately changed the subject. About ten seconds later, her eyelid fluttering slowed and finally stopped. When I mentioned this to my wife afterward she said it was probably because someone in the woman's immediate family had recently come out as being gay.

Winking

Winking is a difficult gesture to interpret, as it has a number of meanings. People who wink too frequently are considered sleazy, and can become the butt of jokes.

A wink is usually meant to be a friendly gesture that is used to create warmth and openness. It can also indicate "okay," or to tell the person that the previous statement was intended to be sarcastic. It sometimes means the two people are sharing a secret, or possibly a private joke. It can also be used to soften an insult or offensive comment by telling the person that "I'm only joking." However, this needs to be interpreted carefully, as the wink may be intended to make the insult worse, rather than better.

Rolling the Eyes

Rolling the eyes upward is a sign of amazement or astonishment. It's a universal gesture used by people all around the world.

Looking Away

When people are anxious, they tend to avoid looking at others. When the situation is normal, these people will make as much eye contact as anyone else. However, they find it hard to make eye contact when the conversation becomes unpleasant or disagreeable. This is likely to be because they're thinking about the negativity that could be created if they put their point of view forward.

Looking away by looking downward is a submissive gesture. There might be times when it's a tactful move to do this. Breaking eye contact with someone with more status and prestige is an example.

Most of the time, it's better to break eye contact by allowing your eyes to drift to one side or the other, or upward. You are still breaking eye contact, but are not allowing yourself to be submissive.

Visual Thinking

The eyes can actually let us get inside a person's mind and determine where an answer is coming from. Is the person remembering it, visualizing it, or constructing it? Here's an example you can try yourself. Look at yourself in a mirror while asking yourself this question: What did your parents give you for your eleventh birthday? There's a 90 percent chance that while thinking about this question your eyes looked upward and to your left. Here's another question. What would the Eiffel Tower look like if it were made from wood? To visualize this, your eyes probably went upward and to the right.

Consequently, it's possible to watch people's eye movements and know where the information they are accessing is coming from. This can be useful in a number of ways.

Eye movements reveal if the person is primarily visual, auditory, or kinesthetic. If you're a salesperson you can use this information to help make a sale by using the language that the person prefers.

Visual thinkers use visual phrases. Consequently, someone who is primarily visual might say something along the lines of "I see," or "that's clear to me."

Auditory thinkers use phrases that relate to sounds. Someone who is auditory might say, "that sounds right," or "that strikes a chord."

Kinesthetic thinkers tend to use more emotional words and phrases. Someone who is kinesthetic might say, "it feels good," or "it's a stretch, but I'm reaching for it."

If you suspect someone is lying, you can ask a few questions and watch the person's eyes to determine where he or she is accessing the information. Once you've determined the eye movements that pertain to him or her, you can start asking questions about the apparent deception. If the person should be remembering something, but is accessing the area where information is being constructed, you have a right to be suspicious.

Approximately 90 percent of right-handed people use the same eye movements. Left-handed people are usually the reverse to right-handed people. However, you need to ask questions to confirm this. Between 5 and 10 percent of people are the opposite of the norm, which is why you always need to ask questions to check how each person operates.

If the eyes go upward and to the person's left, he or she is visually remembering something. An example might be, "What color was the kitchen door in the house you grew up in?"

If the eyes go upward and to the person's right, he or she is visualizing something new, or seeing something familiar in a different way. An example might be, "What would a dog look like if it had huge, rubbery human lips?"

If the eyes go sideways to the person's left, he or she is remembering a sound that has been heard before. An example might be, "What does the ring tone on your cell phone sound like?"

If the eyes go sideways to the person's right, he or she is constructing sounds that have not been heard before. An example might be, "What would a mermaid's singing voice sound like?"

If the eyes go downward and to the person's left, he or she is saying something to him or her self. An example might be, "Where did I leave my car keys?"

If the eyes go downward and to the person's right, he or she is feeling emotions or the sense of touch. An example might be, "What does it feel like to be in love?"

It can be helpful to deliberately move your eyes into the right position when asking yourself a question. If, for instance, you look downward and to the left while asking yourself where you left your car keys, the answer will come back to you more quickly.

The Nose

Traditionally, touching the nose is considered a sign of deceit. It can be, but almost as often, people who are evaluating or considering something touch, rub, or stroke their noses. Someone once told me that when someone is stroking their nose, they're wondering if they can "smell a rat."

People who are thinking something over frequently tap or stroke the tip of their noses. Consequently, this gesture can be a sign that they're about to make a decision.

Touching, rubbing, or pinching the nose can be a sign that the person doesn't believe what the other person is saying. If the person touching his or her nose is the one who is talking, it's a sign that he or she could be lying.

People sometimes pinch their nostrils between the thumb and forefinger of one hand when they hear something unpleasant, or receive bad news. This is a sign that what they've heard is so bad it smells terrible.

Nose Raised

A raised nose is the opposite to chin lowering. When the nose is raised, the person feels full of confidence. He or she may also be feeling critical, judgmental, or superior. Although it's done subconsciously, it can also show the person is demonstrating his or her superiority and snobbery.

Looking Down the Nose

It is a sign of disdain and contempt to look down one's nose, while at the same time half closing the eyes.

Flaring Nostrils

Flaring nostrils is a sign that the person is aroused. The nostrils of lovers flare in anticipation of the delights ahead. However, nostrils also flare when the person has made up his or her mind to do something physical. Once the decision has been made, the nostrils flare to allow as much oxygen as possible into the blood.

This is useful if the person is preparing to move a piano, or has to climb several flights of stairs. However, it can also be a sign of potential danger. Flaring nostrils can be a sign that the person may be about to attack you.

Nose Twist

If someone doesn't believe or approve of what someone else is saying, he or she might momentarily twist the nose to one side. In a sense, these people "smell" something that is not right. This can sometimes also be a gesture of dislike.

Nose Thumb

A mild form of insult is to place the tip of a thumb on the end of your nose, fan the fingers, and wiggle them. I remember doing this as a child and had almost forgotten it until recently,when I saw a woman do it to a group of workmen who were ogling her.

The Ears

If someone rubs an ear between his or her thumb and forefinger, it's a sign that the person doesn't want to hear what is being said. This person is either not interested, or doesn't believe what he or she is being told.

If someone scratches behind an ear with his or her forefinger, it's a sign that he or she is puzzled, perplexed, or has doubts about what has been said.

People sometimes cover their ears to let the speaker know that they don't want to hear any more. This may be because the subject is too distressing, or they've simply heard enough.

A more emphatic way of saying you've had enough is to place a finger inside an ear, and then wiggle it. If someone does this when you're trying to sell him or her something, it's time to pause and rethink your strategy.

Rotating a forefinger in front of the ear is a sign that someone or something is crazy or deranged.

The Cheeks

Cheek Kiss

The cheek kiss is a popular greeting, as it is affectionate but avoids any possible sexual connotations that kissing on the mouth might create. In some places the kiss is on one side only, but it is also frequently performed by kissing one cheek, and then the other.

Slapping the Cheek

When people do something silly they sometimes playfully slap their cheek, as if punishing themselves for their mistake.

Resting the Cheek on a Hand

Resting the cheek on one hand is a sign of tiredness, and tells other people that the person has had enough.

The Mouth

The eyes find it hard to lie, but the mouth can and frequently sends out false information. Consequently, you need to be careful when interpreting nonverbal messages using the mouth alone.

The Mouth at Rest

If you walk down a busy street and look at the people walking toward you, you'll notice a wide range of facial expressions. Except for people who are thinking of something important or humorous, most people will be wearing a habitual expression that can be noticed mainly in the mouth.

Of course, everyone's mouth forms a large variety of expressions every day. However, over a period of time, one expression in particular will become habitual, and this can be interpreted. Habitual lip positions provide a strong clue to deciphering the person's character. Even when the person changes expression, a trace of his or her habitual expression will remain, and this can be interpreted.

If the mouth is loose and slack, the person will be easy to get along with, but will also be indecisive and easily influenced by stronger people.

If the mouth is straight and firm, the person will be conscientious, reliable, and stable.

If the mouth curves upward at the corners, creating a trace of a smile, the person will be easy going, fun loving, and easily pleased. He or she will be an optimist.

If the mouth curves downward at the corners, the person will be strong willed, unsatisfied, easily displeased, and will tend to blame others for anything that goes wrong. He or she will be a pessimist.

True and False Smiles

It takes sixty-four muscles to frown, but only thirteen to smile. A smile is much more powerful than a frown, and takes considerably less effort to produce. Even blind people can hear a smile, as they can detect it in the voices of people who are smiling.

We tend to associate smiles with happiness, but people have different smiles for different purposes. There is the apologetic smile that we use all day long whenever we accidentally interact with someone else. If we accidentally bump into someone at the railway station, we'll say "sorry," and smile. If we squeeze into a crowded elevator, we'll probably avoid eye contact with anyone, but will smile to effectively apologize for forcing everyone to stand closer together. In a busy city, the average person might have dozens of similar encounters during the course of the day. This all-purpose smile is not, however, a genuine one.

Some people make a brief smile at the end of almost every sentence when they are talking to others. This is a nervous smile that tells others that the person is not feeling confident or is not sure of him- or herself.

Smiles can also be used to cover up other feelings and emotions. The person who loses the final of an important tennis tournament will smile bravely to conceal his true feelings. People, who deal with the public all day, every day, use smiles to make their dealings with others more pleasant. Cabin attendants use smiles in this way, but their smiles are also intended to reassure any passengers who are afraid of flying. All of these smiles are useful, and serve a purpose, but they are not genuine smiles.

In the late 1960s, a group of researchers in Birmingham, England, recorded a number of different smiles.[12] The first of these was a simple smile, which is a gentle smile with the teeth unexposed. This occurs when someone is smiling to him- or herself.

The second smile occurs when people meet each other. The upper incisors are visible, and the two people usually make eye-to-eye contact.

The third smile is called a broad smile. This occurs when people are having fun, and are smiling as well as laughing. In this smile, both the upper and lower incisors are visible, and eye-to-eye contact is rare.

The fourth smile is called an oblong smile, which people use when they are being polite. The lips stretch to create an oblong shape. It is also used when people pretend they are enjoying themselves.

The fifth smile is the "how-do-you-do" smile, which is used when meeting strangers. The lips curve upward, and the mouth is slightly open, revealing the upper incisors.

An exaggerated smile, which does not involve the eyebrows, is used to conceal fear and anxiety.

About one hundred and fifty years ago, in 1862, a French neu-
rologist named Guillaume-Benjamin-Amand Duchenne de Boulogne
(1806–1875) conducted a series of tests to find out how a fake smile
differed from a genuine smile. He electrically stimulated various facial
muscles and took photographs of the various muscular contractions
that were produced. He found that a fake smile was produced by the
zygomatic major muscle that runs from the cheekbones to the corners
of the lips. This muscle pulled the lips sideways and upward, creating
a fake smile. A genuine smile was caused by the actions of the zygomatic major muscle and the orbicularis oculi muscle, which surrounds
the eyes. Duchenne wrote: "The emotion of frank joy is expressed on
the face by the combined contraction of the zygomaticus major muscle and the orbicularis oculi. The first obeys the will but the second is
only put in play by the sweet emotions of the soul." [13]

In other words, a genuine smile crinkles the outer edges of the
eyes, raises the cheeks, and activates the outer edges of the mouth. It
is a wonderful gift to receive a genuine smile. It's contagious, and if
you receive one, the chances are you'll feel happy, and will return it.

A fake smile activates only the outer edges of the mouth. It's hard
to fake a genuine smile. Most people have a social smile that they use
with people they are not particularly close to, and reserve their genuine smiles for the people they care about.

Amazingly, even babies can produce social and genuine smiles,
as an experiment involving thirty-five babies demonstrated. The
researchers discovered that a ten-month-old baby could smile at a
stranger without using the muscles around the eyes. However, when
the baby's mother comes into view he or she will produce a genuine
smile.[14]

You can easily discern a fake smile on anyone by observing them
for a while first, and noticing how they greet others. Most people
will receive a fake smile, but the ones the person genuinely likes will
receive a genuine smile.

Knowledge of this lets you know how that person feels about you. You'll also be able to determine how seriously your ideas are being considered. If you receive a fake smile, it might pay to forget about that particular idea, and pursue a different course.

In 1906, Dr. Israel Waynbaum, a French physiologist, found that if someone deliberately smiles, he or she would quickly feel more positive and happy. In the same way, deliberately frowning creates negative feelings. Robert Zajonc (1923–2008), emeritus professor of psychology at Stanford University, rediscovered this research, and suggested that because smiling is related to feelings of happiness, deliberately smiling encourages the brain to release positive neurotransmitters that make the person feel happier. He wrote: "Requiring people to smile, no matter how they really feel at first, results in increased positive feelings; frowning conversely decreases positive feelings." [16]

Closed-Mouth Smile

People who want to dominate others smile seldom. When they are forced to smile they use two types of closed-mouth smiles. The first is a sealed smile. This smile is one in which the lips are kept together while the corners of the mouth are stretched sideways. This type of smile can be frustrating for others, as it's impossible to tell if the person is really smiling. In a sense, this person is keeping his or her true feelings hidden behind the smile.

The second closed-mouth smile is the clamped smile. In this smile the muscles around the mouth are tensed, creating the impression that the person was going to smile, but has managed to hold it back.

People also use closed-mouth smiles when they don't want to reveal their true feelings. If someone says to you, "Don't worry about it," and then gives you a closed-mouth smile, you probably should worry about it. This person is concealing his or her frustration or annoyance by giving you a closed-mouth smile.

Laughter

Laughter is a spontaneous expression of amusement that occurs when something funny happens. Laughter is infectious, and once one person starts laughing, everyone else joins in.

Laughter can also be a powerful weapon. This occurs when someone laughs *at* someone, rather than *with* him or her. Some people can accept this with good grace, but others feel hurt and humiliated when they feel people are laughing at them.

Lips

Lips come in two main types: thick and thin. People with thick lips appear warmer, friendlier, gentler, and more sensual. People with thin lips, on the other hand, are perceived as being colder, stronger, firmer, and lacking in emotion. This explains why women with thin lips often apply lipstick beyond the line of the lip. It makes them appear more sensual and approachable.

Lip Pursing

Pursing the lips occurs when the lips are puckered. This shows the person disagrees, or is concerned about something the other person is saying. If you're trying to sell something to someone and see his or her lips purse, you'll know that you've said something that the customer didn't like or didn't agree with. You'll have to backtrack, clarify the situation, and spend more time answering the person's unspoken questions before carrying on with the sales process.

Lip Compression

People press their lips together when they're under stress. This is not done consciously, but occurs when the person is concerned or worried about something. If the person is suffering severe stress and anxiety, in addition to tightly compressed lips, the corners of his or her mouth will turn down.

Lip Licking

There are many reasons why people lick their lips. It might be a sign of nervousness, as people's mouths get dry when they are stressed or tense. They may be telling a lie. Some people, especially smokers, have dry lips and tend to lick them frequently. Lip licking can also be a flirtatious gesture.

Lip Biting

Biting the lips is a sign of anxiety. When either lip is held by the teeth the person is restraining him- or herself from saying something that might prove embarrassing. In addition, this person is gaining comfort from the support provided by the teeth. Princess Diana was often photographed biting her lips. This revealed her anxiety, and possibly anger, at the attentions of the paparazzi.

Placing Objects in the Mouth

The urge to put something in the mouth occurs frequently when people are anxious. Chewing gum, cigarettes, the ends of spectacles, and a thumb are examples of common objects that are used in this way to reduce anxiety. Sometimes people bite a fingernail for the same reason. I'm a football fan, and find it fascinating to watch Sir Alex Ferguson, manager of the Manchester United Football Club, chewing gum during a game. When everything is going well for his team, he'll chew slowly and steadily. However, the speed and pressure increase markedly when his team is under pressure.

Covering the Mouth

We are all taught to cover our mouths when coughing or sneezing. Likewise, many people cover their mouths to prevent them from saying something they might regret later on. If the fingers are spread and then placed over the mouth, the person is effectively "sieving" the words as he or she speaks.

Covering the mouth, or touching the lips, can also be a sign that the person is lying.

Covering the mouth is often also done as a semi-humorous gesture. After saying something that they shouldn't have, people often place a hand over their mouths, as if they were trying—too late—to stop the words from coming out.

In many Asian countries it's considered rude to reveal the inside of the mouth. Consequently, many Asians cover the mouth when they are smiling or laughing.

Sneer

The sneer can be found all around the world, and is always considered a sign of derision and scorn. A sneer is created when muscles on the sides of the face contract, making the lip corners stretch out toward the ears. The lips often curl as well. Often a sneer lasts for just a moment, and is a sign that the person has no respect for you, and considers you and your ideas worthless. Sometimes the person deliberately keeps the sneer in place, which clearly shows his or her disdain, dislike, and contempt.

Sarcasm

A distorted, one-sided smile that causes the cheek to pucker is a sign that the person is pretending to agree with what he or she is hearing, but is actually feeling contempt.

An asymmetric smile is also a sign that the person is paying no attention to what is being said.

Yawning

Most people consider yawning to be a sign of boredom, and sometimes this is exactly what it is. If someone is performing a repetitious task, or putting up with a lengthy wait for service, he or she is likely to yawn.

However, people also yawn when they're feeling tense, nervous, or facing a difficult challenge. These are known as stress yawns, and they serve a useful purpose as they temporarily distract the person from his or her anxiety.

There is also the threatening yawn. Dominant people use this type of yawn when they want to assert, or regain, their authority.

Laughter

People usually laugh because they are amused. However, people also laugh when they're anxious. The classic example of this was the Milgram Experiment, a controversial study in obedience, conducted in the early 1960s by Dr. Stanley Milgram (1933–1984), a professor at Yale University. Paid volunteers who agreed to take part in the experiments were taken to a laboratory where an experimenter was teaching someone how to remember a list of words. The volunteers were told to encourage and train the student by administering electrical shocks. Although the volunteers weren't aware of it, the experimenter and student were paid actors, and the student, despite his screams and actions, such as banging on the wall, received no shocks. Every time the student made a mistake, the volunteer had to increase the voltage.

Surprisingly, twenty-six of the forty volunteers were willing to send electric shocks of up to 450 volts to the learner, despite hearing his cries of distress in the next room. However, even though they were prepared to deliberately send electric shocks to the learner, many of the students were unhappy about the situation, and about a third of them laughed and smiled when they heard the "learner" screaming and calling for help.

When they were asked about their laughter later, none of the volunteers could explain it. It appeared that they were laughing at the student's distress, but in fact the laughter was a nervous reaction to what they were doing.[17]

The Tongue

The tongue can be extremely revealing in determining what is going on in someone's mind. If someone is stressed, for instance, the mouth will be dry, and the person's tongue will lick his or her lips to moisten them. Interestingly, we all pacify and soothe ourselves by rubbing our tongues from side to side, as this calms us down.

If someone is focused intently on a task, he or she might poke the tip of his or her tongue into a cheek, or slightly out of the mouth. This unconscious action soothes the person while he or she works.

Children, and more than a few adults, all around the world poke out their tongues to annoy and provoke people they are not getting along with.

Clenched Jaws

People tend to clench their jaws when they're feeling angry or tense. However, some people have permanently clenched jaws, showing that they're constantly angry, stressed, or tense.

Jaw Dropping

When people are surprised, disbelieving, aghast, shocked, stunned, perplexed, uncertain, or dismayed, their jaws tend to drop momentarily. Some people deliberately drop their jaws for effect, and keep them lowered for longer than would be the case if the surprise were genuine. This gesture can be disregarded, as it is purely an affectation.

Chin Jut

Jutting the chin is a minor act of aggression usually performed by one male to another. It tells the other person to stand back, or not interfere.

Chin Stroking

This is a common gesture in meetings. As people start assessing what has been said, they often stroke their chins with their thumb and forefinger. This is a sign that they're making a decision. If this occurs during a sales pitch, it's important for the salesperson to stop the sales process until the chin stroking is over. The expressions and gestures the person makes after the chin stroking tell the sales person if the decision is positive or negative.

Blushing

Blushing occurs in moments of shame or embarrassment, or when someone is caught saying or doing something he or she knows is wrong. People also blush when in the company of someone they secretly like. As blushing is totally involuntary, it clearly reveals the person's emotional state.

I knew a man who blushed every time he exaggerated or told a lie. It caused him enormous problems, as he was forced to tell the truth, even in situations when it would have been more diplomatic to lie. As well as blushing, he would start sweating profusely, and frequently left functions early because of the embarrassment this caused him.

Blanching

Blanching is the opposite of blushing. When someone blanches, his or her face turns pale. This occurs when someone experiences a sudden shock, such as a car accident or hears some distressing news. It's a sign of sudden extreme stress.

Blanching is caused by the involuntary nervous system channeling the person's blood to enable him or her to either escape or attack. This must have been useful in the past, but in today's world it makes stress worse, as usually there is nothing the person can do to alleviate the situation.

Disapproval

There are a number of facial expressions that indicate disapproval. Rolling the eyes is a common one. Shaking the head slowly from side to side is another one. Crinkling the nose is a sign of dislike and non-agreement. Usually, it lasts a matter of moments and can easily be missed. However, it's an extremely accurate indicator of what the person is thinking.

The Chin and Jaws

The lower part of the face can be surprisingly revealing in determining people's emotional states.

Anger

People who are angry jut their chins forward. Recently, I picked up my granddaughter from preschool and saw two small boys having an argument. Both of them had jutted their chins forward to emphasize their anger. Adults unconsciously use this gesture when they are angry or feel wronged.

Chin Lowering

The common expression "Keep your chin up" is said to people who look sad or downhearted. It's a reliable indicator of how people feel, as when your chin is lowered you feel a lack of confidence and think negative thoughts. People commonly lower their chin when they're stressed or troubled.

Boredom

It's a sign of boredom when someone uses a hand to support his or her chin. The person is trying to focus on whatever is going on, and supports their chin to help him or her concentrate.

Concentration

This is the opposite of chin support. When someone strokes his or her chin gently, as if it were a beard, it's a sign that he or she is listening carefully to whatever is being discussed.

Clenched Jaw

A clenched jaw is a sign that the person is uncomfortable and feeling ill at ease. It can be a sign of nervousness.

The Neck

People scratch their necks when they're doubtful about something. Consequently, if you tell someone something that is manifestly incorrect, and he or she scratches his or her neck, you'll know that you haven't got away with it.

Protective Gestures

There are five main protective gestures, and they can be seen all around the world.

Covering the eyes with a hand or hands protects the person by preventing him or her from seeing whatever is causing the distress.

Covering the mouth protects the person from saying something he or she might later regret.

Covering the entire face with both hands combines the first two protective gestures. With the entire face covered, the person can't see what is going on, and also can't comment on the distressing event.

Clasping the top of the head with both hands provides symbolic protection, as it shields the head from psychological damage when something distressing occurs. I saw an example of this recently at a golf game. Someone missed an easy putt, and several people who were watching immediately placed their hands on top of their head.

Instead of placing the hands on top of the head, the person may place both hands behind his or her head. This is a form of self-nurturing, and imitates the actions a mother performs when supporting the head of a young baby. This should not be misinterpreted for a similar gesture in which the hands are clasped behind the head, but the elbows are pulled outward. This is a threatening gesture, intended to make the person look bigger and more dangerous.

Deadpan Expression

A deadpan expression is another method people use to protect themselves. Normally, people's faces are animated and lively. Consequently, it can be surprising to see someone with dead eyes and lifeless facial muscles. This expression shows that the person has given up, and simply wants the situation to end.

Sometimes people who are upset or angry put on a deadpan expression, so others won't know just how annoyed and irritated they are.

At one time I did a series of workshops inside a prison. Many of the inmates had deadpan expressions that they used to make them appear nonthreatening and invisible to others.

Another place where you see deadpan expressions are in crowded situations, such as an elevator, train, or bus. In these situations, people put on a deadpan expression, move as little as possible, and avoid eye contact.

Clusters

In this chapter we've looked at a number of gestures and expressions in isolation. In reality, it's impossible to tell what someone is feeling from a single expression or gesture, as they can be interpreted in many different ways. It's not necessarily a sign of lying if someone touches his nose while talking to you. He might simply have an itchy nose. Consequently, it's important to observe the person for a while to see if you can gain any other clues. A series of facial "tells" are known as "clusters."

Would you think someone had good intentions if they approached you with narrowed eyes, lowered eyebrows, and no smile? This person is certainly not being friendly, and is trying to dominate or intimidate you.

If you watch some of the old Clint Eastwood Western movies, you'll see that the people he portrayed use this facial expression regularly.

If someone is extremely anxious, he or she might cough, swallow, and bite his or her lips. There may well also be an urge to put something in the mouth, such as chewing gum, a cigarette, the end of a pen or pencil, or a thumb.

Would you trust someone who looked directly at you, had an animated face, sparkling eyes, and gave you a genuine smile?

Let's assume you're talking with someone you met at a party. As you speak, he assumes a deadpan expression, and looks to one side of you, and then the other. After a minute, he puts his hand up to his mouth to stifle a yawn, and then sighs. You don't need to know anything about facial expressions to know that he's not interested in spending time with you, and is rejecting you in a deliberately open way.

Your Face Can Improve Your Life

You can use the secrets of reading facial expressions to make more friends, become more successful, and gain more pleasure from life. Here are three simple things you can do that will make life smoother, easier, and much more fun:

Make good eye contact with others. People trust people who use eye contact correctly.

Smile. If you look happy, you'll make other people happy. A genuine smile always generates good responses from others

Nod approval. When you nod your head you encourage others, and demonstrate that you're interested in what they have to say.

Most people are unaware of the nonverbal signals they send out, both positive and negative. Once you start paying attention to your habitual signals, you can change them if necessary to convey the image you wish to project.

A restaurateur I knew increased his turnover almost overnight after a friend told him that he always looked grumpy and should smile more. His dour expression did not reflect his true feelings, as he was a happy, contented man. All the same, he discovered that he felt even better about himself and his life once he put a smile on his face.

Reading facial expressions can help you in many ways. People will enjoy communicating with you, as you'll know the right responses to make to what you hear. You'll be able to calm down stressed or angry people before they become aggressive. You'll have a hidden edge in all your personal dealings with others, as you'll be able to read their body language. All of this increases your people skills. This increases your confidence, and makes it much easier for you to achieve your goals.

In the next chapter we'll discuss how to use this knowledge to determine when someone is being dishonest, and lying to you.

When the eyes say one thing and the tongue another, a practiced
man relies on the language of the first.
—RALPH WALDO EMERSON

chapter 13

SIGNS OF DECEPTION

Most people are good at lying but are bad at detecting lies told to them by others. Numerous research studies have revealed that most people can detect deliberate lying slightly more than fifty percent of the time. This gives habitual liars a huge advantage, as they know their lies will be successful much of the time.

The average person lies several times a day. Most of these lies are said to save the feelings of other people, and make life smoother for everyone concerned. If someone is showing off her new dress, and asks you if you like it, you're bound to say "yes," even if you hate it. Likewise, you'll probably thank someone for a delicious meal, no matter how bad it may have been.

Sometimes people lie because they're afraid of the consequences if they tell the truth. This is a form of self-protection. If you were supposed to have a certain task finished on a certain day, but haven't completed it, you might prevent an argument or bad tempers by saying that it's finished.

People lie to protect close friends or family members. If a close friend was accused of something, you might tell others that he's innocent, even though you know he's not.

Work lies are extremely common. You might call a company and ask to speak to someone. That person's secretary tells you "he's not in the office" or is "tied up in a meeting." This might be true, or it could be a lie, if the person wants to avoid speaking to you. You might call a company enquiring about the item you ordered. Someone will tell you: "It was couriered to you yesterday." This may be true, or it could be a delaying tactic.

People frequently lie to bolster their self-image, especially if they don't feel successful enough. A man I used to know told people he met that he was an airline pilot, when he was, in fact, a cabin attendant. I knew a lady who claimed to have written a series of historical novels. She wanted to be a writer, but built herself up by claiming to have already done what she still hoped to accomplish.

People lie frequently when they're trying to impress someone they've just met, especially if it's a potential romantic relationship. They even lie when they end the relationship. "I'll call you" must be one of the most commonly used lies of all.

Many people are bad liars and give themselves away in many different ways. However, some people are extremely good at lying and won't hesitate to lie if it helps them get what they want. Skilled liars are convincing, and can make you believe that they are happy or sad. You need to be alert to pick up the signs that they are telling lies.

There are a number of facial clues that can help uncover a lie.

Expressions

Micro-Expressions

Micro-expressions are genuine expressions that cross the person's face in under one-fifth of a second. Sometimes they are so rapid, you're scarcely aware that you saw them. Someone might be smiling at you, but if for a fraction of a second he or she revealed a look of anger, you'd know the person was feigning the smile. This might, for instance, be a clue that the person doesn't like you, even though he or she appears friendly.

Suppressed Expressions

Suppressed expressions appear more frequently, and last longer, than micro-expressions. As soon as they become aware of it, or when it suits them, these people will replace the suppressed emotion with the expression they want you to see.

About ten years ago, there was a famous murder case in my country in which the apparently grieving husband appeared distraught and devastated whenever there was an audience or a camera around. However, he dropped this façade as soon as he thought he was out of the public eye.

Leakage

Leakage occurs when someone says one thing, but his or her body and face say something else. A common example of this is when someone says he or she agrees with you, but at the same time his or her head shakes slightly, subconsciously proclaiming disagreement. Micro-expressions and suppressed expressions are also examples of leakage.

Facial Muscles

Most of the facial muscles can be consciously controlled. However, the muscles in the forehead and eyebrows can usually provide clues about what people really feel, as they are much harder to manipulate consciously.

If, for instance, someone has wrinkles in the center of his or her forehead, created by the inner corners of the eyebrows rising, he or she will be sad.

If the eyebrows are raised and move toward each other, the person is worried or afraid.

Fake Smiles

In the last chapter we discussed real and false smiles. Liars regularly use smiles to convey emotions that they aren't, in fact, feeling. It can be an interesting exercise to look at photographs of people in newspapers and magazines and determine which smiles are genuine, and which ones aren't. If you're not sure, cover up the bottom half of the face and look at the person's eyes and upper cheeks.

Blinking

People blink more when they're anxious, or under stress. The normal amount of blinking is about fifteen blinks a minute. If someone starts blinking much more than that, it's a sign they're under stress, but are they lying?

Researchers at Portsmouth University in the UK have discovered that good liars stay as motionless as possible, and control their blinking. People tend to make fewer movements when they are thinking hard, and liars need to think harder than most. Dr. Samantha Mann, a psychologist at Portsmouth University, said: "People expect liars to be nervous and shifty and to fidget more, but our research shows that is not the case." She also found that when suspects in police interviews lied they had more pauses in their speech, and also blinked 18.5 times a minute. When they were telling the truth they blinked at 23.6 times a minute.[1] Practiced liars obviously don't feel guilty, stressed, or have a fear of being found out.

Interestingly, O. J. Simpson had a low blink rate when he was on trial for murdering his wife and Ron Goldman. Bill Clinton also had a low blink rate when telling the world he did not have a sexual relationship with Monica Lewinsky.[2] However, former Senator John Edwards started blinking rapidly when he denied he was having an affair.[3]

It seems that a lowering of the blinking rate is a good indication as to whether or not someone is lying. However, an increase in the blinking rate should be considered, too, as, at the least, this is a sign of increased stress and anxiety.

A change in the blinking rate is a better indicator of lying than eye contact. People tend to think that liars find it hard to look others in the eye when they're lying. However, the opposite seems to be the case, as many liars increase their eye contact when telling lies.

Ralph V. Exline (1922–1993), formerly professor of psychology at the University of Delaware, conducted a famous experiment on honesty. Students were placed in pairs and told they were participating in an experiment on decision-making. Although the students didn't know it, one of the "students" was secretly working with the experimenter. Halfway through the test, the experimenter would leave the room. As soon as he did, the fake student would suggest to his partner that they cheat on the test.

Naturally, a number refused, but many of them agreed to cheat. When the experimenter returned and the test continued, he pretended to become worried about how well the two students were doing. Eventually, he told them their results were impossible, and he accused them of cheating.

Before the experiment began, the students had filled out a form that rated them as "low Machiavellians" (straightforward, frank, honest, and caring) or "high Machiavellians" (cunning, crafty, devious, conniving, and opportunistic). The students who had rated themselves as "low Machiavellians" looked away from the experimenter when they lied. However, the "high Machiavellians" made good eye contact with the experimenter when they lied. In fact, they actually increased eye contact.[4]

Inconsistency

It's often a sign of deceit if someone suddenly does something different than he or she has been doing up until then. If, for instance, someone has been sitting calmly, and then rubs his nose or tilts his head before answering a controversial question, the sudden inconsistency is a warning that he might be about to lie.

Another example might be someone who has made regular eye contact, but then, for no apparent reason, tilts their head downward and focuses on the floor.

Asymmetry

Genuine emotions are usually revealed on the face symmetrically. Contempt, in which one side of the mouth is curled, is the single exception. Interestingly, when people deliberately make an expression, it's often asymmetrical. The smile might be crooked, for instance, or one nostril might be slightly raised or flared.

Head Averted

I used to think it was always a sign of a potential lie if someone turned his or her head away while talking to someone. My feelings changed somewhat when I met a man who was slightly deaf. With most conversations, he would turn his head to one side in an attempt to hear better. People who are primarily auditory also turn their heads to one side from time to time.

However, I'm still suspicious if people have made good eye-to-eye contact and then turn their heads to look away while speaking.

Giveaway Signs in the Face

Facial indications should be interpreted in a group, or cluster. If, for instance, someone rubs, strokes, or touches his nose during a conversation, he might be trying to conceal something, or he could have an itchy nose. Bill Clinton touched his nose often while stating that he had not had sex with "that woman." Interestingly enough, neurologists Dr. Alan Hirsch and Dr. Charles Wolf of the Smell and Taste Treatment and Research Foundation found that when people lie their hearts pump faster, and this makes the capillaries in the nose expand. The nose hairs are also affected, and this creates a desire to rub the nose. Although it's not visible, the nose temporarily increases in size. This is known as the "Pinocchio Effect."

Liars usually do one of two things with their eyes. They may avoid eye contact, and not look at you while they're speaking. Alternatively, they'll stare directly at you, with little or no breaks of eye contact. Another clue is that the pupils in the eyes of liars often dilate.

Two researchers, R. E. Lubow and Ofer Fein, found that they could detect guilty people 70 percent of the time by measuring the size of their pupils in photographs taken at the scene of the crime. They also found they could eliminate innocent people 100 percent of the time.[5]

They may cover their mouths with their fingers or palms. This may be a subconscious attempt to prevent you from seeing the lie come out of the person's mouth. Some liars touch or pull on an ear. This could be a subconscious attempt to avoid hearing the lie. Rubbing an eye could mean the person doesn't want to see what happens as a result of the lie.

Many people swallow immediately before saying a lie. This is usually easier to detect in men as their Adam's apple moves.

People who feel guilty about telling the lie often blush. This is due to an increase in body temperature caused by the feelings created by telling the lie. Often, people who don't blush may loosen or fiddle with their collars to release the buildup of heat.

Silence

A former policeman told me that he found silence a potent weapon in unmasking liars. After someone told him something that he doubted, he'd simply stare at the person with a look of disbelief on his face. If the person was lying, he or she usually became uncomfortable. If the person were telling the truth, he or she would become frustrated or angry (compressed lips, lowered eyebrows, narrowed eyes).

The Head

Many liars accompany their words with frequent nods. This is an attempt to get the other person to accept the lie.

Often the entire body, except for the head, is kept still. This is easy to spot, as the only part that moves is the head, which moves slowly from side to side.

When people lie they usually want to touch their face.

The Eyes

Most people find it hard to look someone in the eye while telling a lie. These unskilled liars will look down, or to one side, and will glance at the person they are lying to only briefly. However, skilled liars have no problems with this, and look directly into the other person's eyes while telling a lie.

Any changes in the amount of eye contact can indicate deception. Usually, people make more eye contact when they're listening than when they're talking. Liars sometimes do the opposite, hoping it will convince you of their honesty and sincerity.

Excessive blinking indicates nervousness, which can be a sign of dishonesty. One slow blink immediately after the lie has been told is another giveaway.

The Mouth

Many liars have a fixed, insincere smile that fails to reach the eyes. They also lick their lips, swallow, or clear their throats frequently. This is because the stress of telling a lie causes them to have a dry mouth.

Smiling or laughing nervously at inappropriate moments is a sign of discomfort, which can mean deception.

The Nose

Many liars gain comfort from touching, stroking, or rubbing their noses. This is the grown-up version of a child covering his or her mouth after telling a lie.

In the next chapter we'll look at how we can make this information practical in a number of different situations.

A woman knows the face of the man she loves
as a sailor knows the open sea.
—HONORÉ DE BALZAC

chapter 14

FACE READING
IN EVERYDAY LIFE

By this stage, I'm sure you've realized how useful your knowledge of people's faces and their facial expressions can be. Hopefully, you're already making use of it in your everyday life. In this chapter, we'll look at a few scenarios to show you just how useful this skill can be.

Sales

The more you know about people, the better you'll be as a salesperson. If you go to a business meeting, for instance, you'll be able to tell who is the decision maker, or the most dominant person. Sometimes this person is obvious. He or she will be the person whom everyone defers to, and will probably also be the person who speaks the most. However, I've attended a number of meetings where this person said little, but watched and took everything in. If I hadn't known anything about face reading, I may have ignored this person, and consequently missed out on the sale.

The decision maker is likely to have prominent cheeks, a strong nose, and a large chin. He or she may not have all of these, but usually at least one of these will be obvious.

Once you've assessed that, look at the three horizontal areas of his or her face and decide which one is the most important.

If the area from the hairline to above the eyebrows is the largest, you'll need to include as much interesting information about the product as possible, as he or she will be fascinated by ideas. Describing the features will not result in a sale with someone like this.

If the area between the top of the eyebrows and the base of the nose is the largest, you'll have to focus on results, and how your product will improve the bottom line. The person will want to know if your product is faster, easier to use, and if it can save the company time and money.

If the area from the base of the nose to the tip of the chin is largest, you'll need to present all the facts, and explain them in an easily understood way. These people are capable, down-to-earth, and practical. They appreciate small talk, and like to take time to examine a proposal.

After examining the three divisions, check out the person's eyebrows. If the eyebrows are curved, you'll need to use emotion in your presentation. If they're straight, you'll want to provide practical information on the benefits you can offer. If the eyebrows are angular, you'll need to ask questions, and focus on the person's responses.

Look at the person's nose. Remember that people with large nostrils are good spenders.

Check the lips. Thin-lipped people are more likely to stick to the business at hand than their thicker-lipped colleagues.

Observe the person's posture and facial expressions. Does he or she look interested? Is he or she maintaining good eye contact? Are the pupils dilated to express interest in the proposition? Is he or she smiling? Frowning? Poker-faced? Is he or she nodding in agreement?

If you're aware of these, you can modify and alter your sales pitch to suit the customer, and your results will improve immeasurably.

Interviews

Interviews can be highly stressful. Fortunately, you can use what you now know to create a positive impression, even if you're feeling nervous.

Walk into the interview room with your chin up, and wearing a genuine, open-lipped smile. This tells the interviewer that you're feeling happy, upbeat, and positive. It subliminally suggests that you're enthusiastic and easy to get along with. It also suggests honesty.

Make good eye contact with the interviewer(s). If you fail to make good eye contact, the interviewer will probably assume that you're nervous, but might just as easily think you're shifty or dishonest. However, it's important that you don't out-stare the interviewer, as that makes you appear aggressive. Instead of staring directly into his or her eyes for lengthy periods of time, allow your eyes to scan the other person's face, keeping your eyes at the person's chin level or above.

Smile, and look the interviewer in the eye while shaking hands.

When you sit down, avoid touching your neck, face, or hair. Sit up straight in the chair.

Pay close attention to the interviewer. When you smile, does he respond with a smile? Does her smile include her eyes? If his eyes glaze over or start to wander while you're answering a question, it's time to stop talking.

Faces at Work

Your body language is just as important at work as it is anywhere else. Your posture, facial expressions, and degree of eye contact play an important part in how your colleagues see you.

At a company I worked for many years ago, the sales director promoted one of the sales representatives to sales manager. It was a surprising choice, as everyone in the company was certain another person would have been offered the position. Months later, at a company function, the sales director told a group of people why he'd made the choice he had.

"Bill always stands tall on his own two feet. Larry's always leaning against something. I thought his leaning showed a lack of energy, so I chose Bill."

No one could deny that he'd made a good choice, but we were all surprised at the time that he'd made the choice by observing the body language of the two candidates.

It's important at work to make good eye contact when talking and listening, to smile, and to keep a pleasing expression on your face. This is not always easy, as everyone has good and bad days.

It can be helpful to observe your body language and facial expressions for a day or two. Do you avert your eyes when speaking with your supervisor? Do you fidget, or constantly touch your nose, while talking to others? Do you stand erect, and walk in a positive manner, knowing exactly where you're going, and why you're going there? Do you look as if you're carrying the world on your shoulders?

Most importantly, do you look happy to be working for this particular company? A cheerful expression makes you more likable, good eye contact makes you more trusted, and an erect posture makes you look physically active.

Flirting

Most people want to share their lives with someone else. Some people find the right person easily, while others spend years wishing and hoping the right person would appear. Flirting is a fun, playful way to express your interest in someone you find attractive. It involves both verbal and nonverbal actions, and should be enjoyable for both people.

I have a friend who is opposed to flirting, as he says it's dishonest. He may not be the best person to pontificate on these matters, as he's in his fifties and is still single. I think fear of rejection and failure has held him back, and because of this, he's probably lost hundreds, if not thousands, of opportunities to meet the woman of his dreams.

Obviously, not everyone you try to flirt with will flirt back, but some will. Like almost everything else, flirting involves taking a risk. Fortunately, you can use your knowledge of face reading and facial expressions to eliminate most of that, while at the same time increasing your enjoyment of life by meeting many more people.

Smiling is the most important thing you can do. It makes you look friendly and approachable. It tells others they can approach you, and you won't reject them. As a bonus, it makes you feel positive, confident, and relaxed.

Of course, the smile has to be genuine. Recently, I had coffee at a café I hadn't been to before, and I was fascinated with the facial expressions of the owner. Each time he delivered food or a drink to a table, he'd do it with a wide smile on his face. That was good, but as soon as he'd completed the task his smile disappeared. It made him look insincere and dishonest. That's the last impression you want to make when you're searching for a partner.

Eye contact is another essential element. If you notice someone looking at you, make direct eye contact for three or four seconds before looking away. Silently count to three, smile, and look at the person again, this time for a second or two. Repeat several times, if necessary. When you feel the interest is mutual, walk over to the person and start a conversation.

Once you start talking, all the usual elements of facial expressions come into play. This person is interested in you if he or she focuses on you, listens to what you say, and makes good responses. If the person starts looking at his or her watch, gazes over your shoulder or around the room, or does anything else to indicate lack of interest, it's time to move on.

With flirting, there's another facial gesture that you need to look for: preening. This is done by both men and women. A man might touch his hair, adjust his tie or shirt collar, rub his chin, or stroke a cheek. A woman might play with her hair, toss her hair, tuck her hair behind her ears, massage her neck, reapply lipstick, play with her earrings, or rearrange an item of clothing.

When I told a friend I was including this section in the book, she said people have to be willing to make the first move. "Most people are too shy to do it," she told me. "You can tell they want to, but they hold back. If you make the first move, you'll get to meet many more people and have much more fun."

Social Situations

Some people love being invited to parties, as it gives them an opportunity to meet people, and possibly make new friends. Other people dread parties, as they fear they might not meet anyone they like, and may end up as "wall flowers."

The people in the first group are probably already using good body language. They smile, make good eye contact, nod their heads when listening, and have an open posture. The body language of the people in the second group tells everyone that they're uncomfortable, nervous, and wish they'd stayed at home. These people have a closed posture (arms folded, hands clasped, or sitting with arms and legs crossed, possibly with a hand covering the mouth and chin), make little or no eye contact, and fail to smile.

If you feel uncomfortable at the idea of going to a social event where you'll know few people, do some research ahead of time. If possible, find out something about some of the people who'll be attending.

Not long ago, I was told that someone who designed wind farms was going to be at a party I was invited to. I looked up wind farms on the Internet and was able to ask her some interesting, and hopefully intelligent, questions about her work.

You should also read a newspaper, or watch a few current affairs programs on TV, to enable you to contribute to the conversation. In addition, you should have a few entertaining comments you can make about your own work, as it's common for people to ask others what they do for a living.

When you get to the party, take a deep breath before going in, place a pleasant smile on your face, stand erect with your head up, and walk in. Keep your arms uncrossed, and your hands away from your face. Start circulating around the room, looking for friendly faces. When you find someone who looks open and friendly, casually walk over and make a compliment, or simply say, Hello. Once the other person has responded, you can introduce yourself, or make a comment about the food, music, size of the crowd, or anything else. Ask questions, and listen to the answers. Reveal something about yourself, and allow the conversation to gradually develop.

If you're at a cocktail party, you can join a group of two or three people who are engaged in conversation. Move close to them, and pay attention to what they're saying. Smile, nod your head, and make plenty of eye contact. When a pause occurs in the conversation, you can make a comment or ask a question. Of course, if you can tell the conversation is a private one, you should move on to another group, as you don't want to intrude into other people's personal lives.

Naturally, you may not "click" with the first person you speak to. In this case, you'll want to end the conversation after a few minutes. You need to do this pleasantly. Make a positive comment on what the person has told you. This tells the person that you have been paying attention. Say you're going to see a friend, or get something to eat or drink. You may offer to get the person another drink. If you do this, you can return with the glass, smile, and move on.

Many people panic at the thought of ending a stilted conversation because they know no one else in the room. If the conversation isn't working, you're better off ending it. Get yourself another drink, or something to eat, and repeat the initial process of looking for a friendly person or an open group.

As long as you keep an open posture, and look happy, you'll find yourself enjoying pleasant conversations with a variety of people, and having a good time. If you do this, you might be surprised to find you're one of the last guests to leave the party.

Playing Poker

I've heard many people joke about refusing to play poker with anyone who wore dark glasses. When conducting business deals, Aristotle Onassis (1904–1975), the Greek shipping magnate, always wore dark glasses, but refused to let anyone else do the same. This is because his dark glasses prevented others from knowing when his pupils dilated. If a gambler is dealt four aces, for instance, he might keep a poker face, but his pupils would dilate to express his pleasure, and give him away. Consequently, even though people laugh about it, you should refuse to play with people who wear dark glasses. It's important to see their eyes.

You'll also need to modify your own natural behavior. It's natural to look pleased when you're dealt a good hand, but when playing poker you're also trying to bluff your opponents. You might look happy when dealt a bad hand, and appear downcast when dealt a good hand. Bluffing is not as easy as it sounds, and many gamblers are constantly trying to improve their bluffing skills. You should also bluff only when you think you have a good chance of getting away with it.

Examine your own body language, and remove any giveaway leaks or other clues you might subconsciously be transmitting to your opponents. Be aware that your opponents may be giving you clues through their subconscious leakages, but they may just as easily be deliberately sending you the wrong information. You need to make sure that their leakages are genuine and are, in fact, leakages.

Be your normal self, as much as possible. If you suddenly change the amount of eye contact you normally use, or start rubbing your nose or scratching an ear, your opponents will notice, and use it to their advantage. A friend of mine has a nervous habit of touching his nose repeatedly. If he suddenly stopped doing this in the middle of a game of poker, it would be suspicious.

Without making it obvious, pay attention to the body language of your opponents. With what you know now, you'll be in a strong position to know exactly what's going on behind the mask or poker face.

As you can see, you'll be able to use what you've learned in this book almost every day. The more you consciously use it, the better you'll become. In time, you'll find yourself using it almost without thinking, as it will simply be something you do in every type of situation.

Alas, after a certain age, every man is responsible for his face.
—ALBERT CAMUS

CONCLUSION

Learning about face reading and facial expressions enhanced my life in many different ways. I'm sure it will do exactly the same for you. You'll find this skill useful in every area of your life. You'll also find yourself making fewer judgments about people based on how they look.

Many years ago, when I was working as a children's entertainer, a teacher at a school I performed at commented on my choice of children to help me onstage.

"All the children you chose were good looking," she told me. "I've noticed they're the children who always get picked. The less attractive kids tend to be overlooked." She then went on to tell me that even teachers believe that neatly dressed, clean, good-looking students are brighter than less attractive students.

"I had to learn that that's not necessarily the case," she continued. "Good-looking people get treated better everywhere, and it starts in childhood. You chose the good-looking children because you thought they'd be smarter and would react better. Why don't you pick a few ugly kids to help you next time, and see what happens?"

This teacher gave me a great deal of food for thought. I knew nothing about face reading or facial expressions at the time, and hadn't been aware that I was choosing the better-looking children. Yet, subconsciously, I had fallen into the trap of thinking they'd be better volunteers. It had also never occurred to me that the children I was choosing were the same children everyone else chose, for the same reasons I had.

I immediately started choosing less-attractive-looking children as my audience volunteers and found they were usually better than the ones I'd picked in the past. These were children who were normally overlooked in this sort of situation. They were grateful at finally being chosen and made excellent volunteers.

This new knowledge was helpful to me in my shows, but I also found it useful in other areas of life, as it taught me to look past people's looks. I had a wonderful man who serviced my car for many years. People used to tell me they'd never go to him, as he looked evil and sinister. At one time, I employed a young artist to illustrate a book I was writing. She was very grateful for the work and told me she found it hard to get work because of a large, unsightly birthmark she had on one cheek. Because it was so obvious, she felt self-conscious and embarrassed every time she tried to get work. These are just two examples of people I might have unjustly rejected in the days before I learned face reading.

I no longer, even subconsciously, think that beautiful women and handsome men have better personalities and are more capable than people who were not blessed with attractive looks. Have you ever noticed how good-looking political candidates usually win over their less good-looking opponents? Good-looking people are sought after, and receive more job offers, more dates, and—as yet another bonus— have sex more often. Yet they are no more honest, intelligent, or kind than anyone else. Knowledge of face reading will help you go well beyond surface appearances, and see the real person underneath.

Of course, I also discovered that this works in reverse. As people subconsciously choose good-looking people, I started paying more attention to my own grooming, especially in situations where I was selling myself and what I had to offer.

I found the same thing occurred when I started studying kinesics, especially facial expressions. It explained many things that had puzzled me for years. For instance, when I was working in publishing in the UK, I had two good friends who were on the same program I was on. At the end of the program, I was transferred to a position in New Zealand, but the other two were both chasing the same editorial position in the company.

Bill was extremely intelligent, and loved everything about the book trade. He was diligent, and worked hard. However, he was shy, hesitant, and self-effacing. He also spoke softly, and this, accompanied by his modest demeanor, meant that people often ignored him when he spoke.

Mark, my other friend, was the total opposite. He had entered publishing because his parents owned a bookstore, and thought it would be good training for him before he ultimately took over the family business. He had the largest collection of jokes of anyone I've ever met, and he loved regaling people with them, whether they wanted to hear them or not. He was loud, enthusiastic, and thought everyone loved him. I was surprised that he wanted an editorial position, as I always thought he should be dealing with the public, because he loved people so much. None of us knew that a third person had also applied for the position. Brendan got on well with everyone. He was considerate, polite, and spoke only when he knew what he wanted to say. He made good eye contact, and had a charming smile. At the time, I was sure Bill would be offered the position, as I thought he was the best person for the job. I suggested to Mark that he should apply for a sales position, but he was adamant he'd be perfect in an editorial role. Much to our surprise, Brendan was offered the position. At the time, I was puzzled about this. Brendan wasn't as intelligent or hard working as Bill, but his body language and ability to get on well with others made him the natural choice for the position.

I'm sure you have experienced similar scenarios, when the person who used kinesics wisely moved ahead of people who knew nothing about it, or failed to use it. Learning to read the hidden language of the face and facial expressions will enable you to "tune in" to other people, and know how their thinking processes work. It will also make you more receptive, sympathetic, and understanding to other people's outlooks and differing points of view.

Rebecca Scholl, a successful face reader, told me that the biggest thing she discovered while learning face reading was that she could improve her own personality and image. She always has a happy smile on her face, but she told me that wasn't always the case. "I used to scowl a great deal," she told me. "One day, while I was studying physiognomy, I looked at myself in a mirror and was horrified at what I saw. I turned my scowl into a smile almost overnight, but it took a long time to eliminate all the signs of worry from my face." Rebecca is almost eighty years old, but looks twenty years younger. She told me: "That's entirely due to the changes I made in my life after seeing myself—really seeing myself for the first time—in that mirror."

Over the years, I've been fortunate enough to meet many eminent face readers. T'ai Lau, who taught me feng shui, was an extremely good face reader. Henry B. Lin, author of *What Your Face Reveals*, is another example. Possibly the most fascinating face reader I've met was a middle-aged American woman named Margaret Lamb who lived in Singapore. I was intrigued that she chose to make her living as a physiognomist in a country that already had a large number of face readers. I met her in 1991 or 1992. After my reading, I invited her out for dinner, as I wanted to learn more about her and her interests.

"Originally, I read auras," she told me. "I did that for many years, first in Philadelphia, and then in Chicago. I know exactly when I started paying attention to people's faces. Up until that day, I'd been so fascinated with people's auras that I didn't pay much attention to their faces. One day I read for a man who was astonishingly ugly, but he had the most beautiful, serene, spiritual aura. I couldn't stop looking at him. Usually, I'm happy for people to leave at the end of their session, but I didn't want this man to go. I just wanted to keep gazing at him. A day or two later, I went to the library and found a book on face reading. It was fascinating, but I didn't do much with it for several years. Then, when my marriage broke up, I decided to go to China to learn face reading. My friends advised me to go to Singapore instead, as they told me I'd be able to find teachers who spoke English. I was lucky, and found a good teacher. I was going to stay three months, but I fell in love with the place, and I'm still here seven years later. I do combined face and aura readings. I don't know if anyone else does this, but it makes perfect sense to me, and my clients seem to enjoy it. Most of my work is for the expats living here. I see some tourists, and a few local Chinese. They come out of curiosity, I think."

I've met many readers who use face reading as a small part of what they offer. Margaret is the only person I've met who combines it with another system. The other readers advertise themselves as palm or Tarot card readers, and include a few minutes on the face.

Most people learn face reading and study facial expressions for their own interest, but there are good opportunities for professional physiognomists. In the East, it's easy to find a face reader, but they're not that common in the West. I'm sure you'd be kept busy if you decided to take up face reading professionally.

Don't try to learn everything about face reading at once. Focus on, say, the eyebrows, for a few days, and then move on to another feature. If you do this for a few weeks, you'll know more than most people will ever know about face reading and facial features. They are both fascinating subjects, and the more you learn about them, the more useful they'll be for you in everyday life. I wish you great success with both of them.

THE HISTORY
OF FACE READING

Despite the saying, "never judge others by their appearance," people have been doing exactly that for millenia. The art of face reading probably began in China about three thousand years ago. There are records describing unusual markings on the faces of some of their earliest emperors, showing that interest in the subject is extremely old.

The oldest existing book on face reading was written by Gui Gu-Tze, a philosopher and teacher, who lived about 2,500 years ago. He is considered the father of Chinese face reading.

Face reading gradually became more and more important in China. During the time of the Tang Dynasty (618–907 CE), a scholar named Zhong Kui gained first place in the imperial examinations. However, as he was considered ugly, the emperor disqualified him, and he committed suicide.

During the time of the Ching Dynasty (1644–1911), people who had failed the Third Degree imperial examinations were accepted if they had suitably propitious faces. These examinations were extremely important, as success in them meant the person could enter official life and enjoy a lucrative career. The propitious faces were: broad and oblong, broad and square, narrow and oblong, and small and oblong.[1]

Physiognomy, divination using facial features, was also popular in ancient Greece, and appears to have started independently from the Chinese tradition. Aristotle (384–322 BCE) wrote a treatise on the subject called *Physiognomonica*. In his *Prior Analytics*, Aristotle wrote: "It is possible to infer character from features, if it is granted that the body and the soul are changed together by the natural affections ... I refer to passions and desires when I speak of natural emotions."[2]

The Arabian philosophers, Averroes (1126–1198) and Avicenna (980–1037), developed Aristotle's ideas. Avicenna explained the art of face reading in his book, *De Animalibus*.

Albertus Magnus (c.1200–1280)—the German philosopher, bishop, and scholar—was the first person in the West to write a book on physiognomy. The first printed book on the subject was *De Hominis Physiognomia* by Michael Scot. It was written in 1272, but did not appear in print until 1477.

During the Middle Ages, physiognomy and palmistry were taught at a university level, until King Henry VIII banned it in 1531.

A number of important books on physiognomy were published in the sixteenth century. These include *Physiognomonia* by Barthélemy Coclès (Strasbourg, 1533), *Physionomie* by Maître Michel Lescot (1540), *Chiromance* by Jean d'Indagine (1549), and *De Humana Physiognomia* (1586) by Gian Battista Della Porta.

Jerome Cardan (1501–1576), also known as Girolamo Cardano, was a French physician, astrologer, gambler, and prolific author. He was an eccentric, flamboyant character who wore an emerald around his neck. He placed this in his mouth whenever he heard bad news. He must have done this frequently, as throughout his life he was attacked by numerous critics and enemies. In addition to this, his son was executed for murdering his wife, and, after the Inquisition accused him of heresy, Cardan spent time in prison. By the time of his death, he had published fifty-four books, and had almost as many manuscripts ready for publication. In addition to this, he had destroyed about 130 other manuscripts that he considered not good enough for publication. His autobiography was not published until 1643. Jerome Cardan developed a method of reading the lines on the forehead. His influential, and extremely popular, book called *Metoposcopia* was finally published in 1658, almost eighty years after his death.

Italian author and playwright Gian Battista Della Porta (1535–1615) tried to modernize physiognomy with his book *De Humana Physiognomia*, published in 1586. He wrote that people's characters and facial features were a result of heredity and temperament, rather than the influence of the planets. Della Porta was ahead of his time in writing this. Unfortunately though, in the same book he compared the faces of people with animals. "Goat-faced men, like the goat, were stupid," is an example. "Lion-faced men were, like lions, strong and fearless," is another. Consequently, his book both updated physiognomy and simultaneously took it several steps backward.

In 1697, John Evelyn, the English essayist, wrote a *Digression concerning Physiognomy*. He put forward the idea that the "spirits of the passions" lived in the brain. By constantly thinking and acting on these passions, the spirits flowed into various nerves on the face, and eventually the features became "unalterably fixt."

Johann Kaspar Lavater (1741–1801), a Swiss Lutheran minister, hymn writer, and poet, wrote a series of articles on physiognomy, which were collected and published in 1772. His *Essays on Physiognomy*, published between 1775 and 1778, was two thousand pages long. This book was originally published in German, and was quickly translated into French. The first English translation, in four volumes, was published in 1804. By 1810, there were sixteen German, fifteen French, two American, one Dutch, and at least twenty English editions of his book in print.[3] His book became a huge publishing success and sold steadily for the next hundred years. It is largely thanks to Lavater's work that many nineteenth-century authors such as Honoré de Balzac, Charles Dickens, Thomas Hardy, and Charlotte Bronte, spent so much time describing the facial characteristics of the characters in their novels.

The Picture of Dorian Gray, by Oscar Wilde, uses aspects of physiognomy, as do many of Edgar Allan Poe's short stories.[4]

Johann Lavater was pastor of St. Peter's, the oldest church in Zurich, from 1788 until his death in 1801, and is buried there. He was killed by a sniper's bullet while tending to the injured during the Napoleonic Wars.

Remarkably, Charles Darwin (1809–1882), author of *The Origin of Species*, was almost refused permission to travel on the *HMS Beagle* because of Johann Lavater. Darwin wrote in his *Autobiography*:

"Afterwards on becoming very intimate with Fitz-Roy [the Captain], I heard that I had run a very narrow risk of being rejected, on account of the shape of my nose! He was an ardent disciple of Lavater, and was convinced that he could judge a man's character by the outline of his features; and he doubted whether any one with my nose could possess sufficient energy and determination for the voyage. But I think he was afterwards well satisfied that my nose had spoken falsely."[5]

In the late 1930s, the Japanese air force used a face reader to study the faces of all new recruits to determine what sort of work they would be best suited for. As a result of this, some would become pilots, for instance, while others might become office workers, mechanics, or navigators.[6]

Physiognomy never entirely disappeared, but fell out of favor for many years. Today it has become popular again as research has shown that certain character traits, such as honesty and aggression, can be easily discerned in the face.

One example of this research is described in a paper written by two psychologists: Anthony C. Little from the University of Stirling and David I. Perrett from the University of St. Andrews. They asked 191 people to complete a questionnaire that measured their degrees of openness, conscientiousness, extraversion, agreeableness, and neuroticism. They took photographs of the men and women who measured highest and lowest in the test, and used a computer to turn the photographs into four single composite images, creating a high-scoring man, a low-scoring man, a high-scoring woman, and a low-scoring woman. The researchers then showed these photographs to forty people, and asked them to rate them on different personality profiles (agreeableness, conscientiousness, extraversion, neuroticism, openness to experience, attractiveness, masculinity, and age). The results were extremely accurate, and people were able to tell which composites were reliable, which were extroverted, and so on. This experiment shows that our personalities are, at least to a certain extent, clearly visible on our faces.[7]

In February 2009 an article in *New Scientist* magazine said: "the field is undergoing something of a revival. Researchers around the world are re-evaluating what we see in a face, investigating whether it can give us a glimpse of someone's personality or even help to shape their destiny." [8]

As well as studying facial features, people have also been investigating body language for thousands of years. Cicero (106–43 BCE), the Roman philosopher, wrote that actions of the body were "the sentiments and passions" of the soul. He realized that communication was made up of words, but thought that posture, facial expressions, and gestures also played a major role.

John Bulwer published his *Chirologia: The Natural History of the Hand* in 1644. This book discussed more than one hundred different hand gestures, and what they meant. Almost two hundred years later, Gilbert Austin's book *Chironomia* (1806) discussed how gestures could be used to make speeches and talks more effective.

Celebrated scientist Charles Darwin (1809–1882) studied humans and apes and was fascinated how both used facial expressions to express their emotions. His book, *The Expression of the Emotions in Man and Animals*, was a milestone in ethology, the study of animal behavior.[9]

Kinesics, the study of body movements, including facial expressions, was developed in the 1950s by Ray L. Birdwhistell (1918–1994), an anthropologist at the Eastern Pennsylvania Psychiatric Research Institute. His first book on the subject, *Introduction to Kinesics*, was published in 1952.[10]

Paul Ekman (born 1934), a psychologist at the University of California, developed this further by studying filmed interviews of psychiatric patients who wanted to be released back into the community. He confirmed the importance of "leakage" in detecting deception.

NOTES

Introduction

1. Agatha Christie, *Murder on the Orient Express* (London: William Collins & Sons, 1934) 22. Published in the U.S. as *Murder in the Calais Coach* (New York: Dodd, Mead and Company, 1934).

Chapter One

1. Donna McIntyre, "Body Language Key to First Impression." Article in *The New Zealand Herald* 6/15/11, B8.

Chapter Three

1. Arcandam was the pseudonym used by the author of a number of books of predictions. The first of these was published in 1541. The author was probably Richard Roussat, a doctor and priest who lived in Lyon, France. He was listed as editor of the first books. The books were originally published in French and Latin. The first English translation appeared in 1562.

Chapter Four

1. Napoleon, quoted in http://www.bartleby.com/78/569.html. Although this quote can be found in many sites on the Internet, I have been unable to verify it. The closest I have found is: "It is narrated of Napoleon that he was a practical Nasologist, and influenced in his choice of men by the size of their Noses." George Jabet, *Notes on Noses* (London: Richard Bentley, 1847), 43.
2. John Liggett, *The Human Face* (London: Constable & Company Limited, 1974), 221.

Chapter Five

1. L. A. Doust, *Looking at Faces* (London: Frederick Warne & Co. Ltd., 1948), 18.
2. Richard Webster, *Communicating with the Archangel Gabriel for Inspiration and Reconciliation* (St. Paul: Llewellyn Publications, 2005), 15.

Chapter Six

1. The full title of Jerome Cardan's book is *Metoposcopia libris tredecim et octingentis Faciei humanae Eicomibus complexa; cui accessis Metampodia de Navis Corporis Tractalus Craecs et Latina nunc primum editus*. It was originally published in Latin by Thomas Jolly in 1658, and a French translation was published later in the same year. Nineteen of the delightful illustrations in *Metoposcopia* can be found in: Émile Grillot de Givry (translated by J. Courtneay Locke), *Illustrated Anthology of Sorcery, Magic and Alchemy* (New York: Causeway Books, 1973), originally published in France in 1929.

Chapter Eight

1. Aristotle, *Displaying the Secrets of Nature Relating to Physiognomy*. Available online at: http://www.readbookonline.net/readOnLine /41021/.

2. Johann Lavater, *Essays on Physiognomy*. Available online at: http://books.google.com/books/about/Essays_on_physiognomy .html?id=HMJDA3k2yOcC.

Chapter Ten

1. Eva Shaw, *Divining the Future: Prognostication from Astrology to Zoomancy* (New York: Facts on File, Inc., 1975), 143.

2. Rama Dayaju Panditudu, *Sanketa Nidhi Prachnina Jyothisya Grandamu*, Slokas ii–25, iv–16, and vi–5. There are many translations of this classic Indian book on astrology. The easiest one to find in the West is published by: New Delhi: Ranjan Publications, 1994. It can also be found online at: http://www .astrovidya.com/Sanketa%20Nidhi.pdf.

Chapter Twelve

1. Sigmund Freud, *Fragments of an Analysis of a Case of Hysteria*, 1905.

2. Ken Cooper, *Nonverbal Communication for Business Success* (New York: AMACOM, 1979), 69–70.

3. Albert Mehrabian, *Silent Messages: Implicit Communication of Emotions and Attitudes* (Belmont, KY: Wadsworth Publishing Company, 1971). See also: http://www.kaaj.com/psych/smorder.html.

4. Nathan J. Gordon and William L. Fleisher, *Effective Interviewing and Interrogation Techniques* (Burlington, MA: Academic Press, second edition, 2006), 83.

5. Jonathan Cole, *About Face* (Cambridge, MA: The MIT Press, 1998), 50.

6. Daniel Goleman, *Emotional Intelligence* (New York: Bantam Books, Inc., 1975), 13–20.

7. Roger E. Axtell, *Gestures: The Do's and Taboos of Body Language Around the World* (New York: John Wiley & Sons, Inc., revised edition, 1998), 65.

8. Paul Ekman, *Emotions Revealed* (New York: Henry Holt and Company, 2003), 14–15.

9. John Nolte, *The Human Brain: An Introduction to its Functional Anatomy* (Philadelphia: Mosby, Inc., 1999), 431–32.

10. Ken Cooper, *Nonverbal Communication for Business Success*, 75.

11. Gordon R. Wainwright, revised by Richard Thompson, *Master Body Language* (London: Hodder Education, 2011), 6.

12. Dilys Hartland and Caroline Tosh, *Guide to Body Language* (London: Caxton Publishing Group Ltd., 2001), 108.

13. G. B. Duchenne de Boulogne (translated and edited by R. Andrew Cuthbertson), *The Mechanism of Human Facial Expression* (New York: Cambridge University Press, 1990), 277–79. (Originally published in French in 1862.)

14. Nathan A. Fox and Richard J. Davidson, "Electroencephalogram Asymmetry in Response to the Approach of a Stranger and Maternal Separation in 10-month-old Children." Article in *Developmental Psychology*, Vol. 23 (2), March 1987, 233–40.

15. Peter Jaret, "Blinking and Thinking." Article in *In Health*, July/August 1990, 4 (4), 36–37.

16. R. B. Zajonc, S. T. Murphy, and M. Inglehart, "Feeling and Facial Efference: Implications of the Vascular Theory of Emotion." Article in: *Psychological Review 96* (1989), 395–416.

17. Stanley Milgram, "Behavioral Study of Obedience." Article in *Journal of Abnormal and Social Psychology 67* (4), 1963, pages 371–78. A much fuller account of this controversial and possibly unethical experiment, along with nineteen variations, can be found in: Stanley Milgram, *Obedience to Authority: An Experimental View* (New York: Harper & Row, Inc., 1974).

Chapter Thirteen

1. Roger Dobson and Ed Habershon, "Liars don't blink: they keep still and concentrate hard." Article in London: *The Sunday Times*, March 19, 2006. Available online at: http://www.timesonline.co.uk/tol/news/uk/article742788.ece.

2. J. J. Teece, "Body Language of Criminals" (February 25, 2009) http://www.bowdoin.edu/visitors-friends/bowdoin-breakfast/pdf/1-body-language.pdf.

3. "How to Tell if Someone is Lying." Unattributed article September 8, 2008. http://abcnews.go.com/GMA/Books/story?id=5747450&page=1.

4. Evan Marshall, *The Eyes Have It: Revealing Their Power, Messages, and Secrets* (New York: Citadel Press, 2003), 18.

5. R. E. Lubow and Ofer Fein, "Pupillary size in response to a visual guilty knowledge test: New technique for the detection of deception." *Journal of Experimental Psychology: Applied*, Vol. 2 (2), June 1996, 164–177.

Appendix

1. Frena Bloomfield, *The Book of Chinese Beliefs* (London: Arrow Books Limited, 1983), 142–43.

2. Aristotle (translated by A. J. Jenkinson), *Prior Analytics*, Part 2:27. Can be found in many places online, including http://ebooks.adelaide.edu.au/a/aristotle/a8pra/.

3. John Liggett, *The Human Face* (London: Constable & Company Limited, 1974), 190.

4. Erik Grayson, *Weird Science, Weirder Unity: Phrenology and Physiognomy in Edgar Allan Poe*. This text can be found online at: http://binghamton.academia.edu/ErikGrayson/Papers/330818/WEIRD_SCIENCE_WEIRDER_UNITY_PHRENOLOGY_AND_PHYSIOGNOMY_IN_EDGAR_ALLAN_POE.

5. Charles Darwin, *The Life and Letters of Charles Darwin* (New York: D. Appleton, 1887), 12. Available online at: http://charles-darwin

.classic-literature.co.uk/the-autobiography-of-charles-darwin/ebook-page-12.asp.

6. Boyé Lafayette De Mente, *Asian Face Reading: Unlock the Secrets Hidden in the Human Face*, (Boston, MA: Journey Books, 2003), 8.

7. A. C. Little and D. I. Perrett, "Using Composite Face Images to assess accuracy in personality attribution." Article in *British Journal of Psychology, 98*, pages 111–26, 2007. Also available online at: http://www.alittlelab.stir.ac.uk/pubs/Little_07_personality_composites.pdf.

8. Roger Highfield, Richard Wiseman and Rob Jenkins, "How Looks Betray Your Personality." Article in *New Scientist* Issue 2695, February 11, 2009. Available online at: http://www.newscientist.com/article/mg20126957.300-how-your-looks-betray-your-personality.html?full=true.

9. Charles Darwin, *The Expression of the Emotions in Man and Animals* (London: John Murray and Company, 1872).

10. Ray L. Birdwhistell, *Introduction to Kinesics* (Louisville: University of Louisville Press, 1952). His best-known book is *Kinesics and Context: Essays on Body Motion Communication* (Philadelphia: University of Philadelphia Press, 1970).

SUGGESTED READING

Alessandra, Tony, and Michael J. O'Connor, with Janice Van Dyke. *People Smarts: Bending the Golden Rule to Give Others What They Want.* San Diego: Pfeiffer & Company, 1994.

Axtell, Roger E. *Gestures: The Do's and Taboos of Body Language Around the World.* New York: John Wiley & Sons, Inc., 1991. Revised and expanded edition, 1998.

Beattie, Geoffrey. *Visible Thought: The New Psychology of Body Language.* Hove and New York: Routledge, 2003.

Birdwhistell, Ray L. *Kinesics and Context: Essays on Body Motion Communication.* Philadelphia: University of Pennsylvania Press, 1970.

Brooks, Michael. *Instant Rapport.* New York: Warner Books, Inc., 1989.

Cole, Jonathan. *About Face.* Cambridge, MA: The MIT Press, 1998.

Collett, Peter. *The Book of Tells: How to Read People's Minds from Their Actions.* London: Bantam Books, 2004.

Darwin, Charles. *The Expression of Emotion in Man and Animals.* London: John Murray, 1872.

De Mente, Boyé Lafayette. *Asian Face Reading: Unlock the Secrets Hidden in the Human Face.* Boston: Journey Editions, 2003.

Douglas, T. S. *Learn to Read Character*. London: Pan Books Limited, 1963.

Drozdeck, Steven, Joseph Yeager, and Linda Sommer. *What They Don't Teach You in Sales 101: How Top Salespeople Recognize and Respond to Nonverbal Buying Signals*. New York: McGraw-Hill, Inc., 1991.

Ekman, Paul. *Emotions Revealed: Recognizing Faces and Feelings to Improve Communication and Emotional Life*. New York: Henry Holt and Company, Inc., second edition 2007. Originally published 2003.

———. *Telling Lies: Clues to Deceit in the Marketplace, Politics, and Marriage*. New York: W. W. Norton & Company, Inc., Reissued with a new chapter 2009. Originally published 1985.

Fast, Julius. *Body Language*. London: Souvenir Press Limited, 1971.

Glas, Norbert (translated by Pauline Wehrle). *Reading the Face: Understanding a Person's Character Through Physiognomy*. Forest Row, UK: Temple Lodge Publishing, 2008. (Originally published in German 1961.)

Gordon, Nathan J., and William L. Fleisher. *Effective Interviewing and Interrogation Techniques*. Burlington, MA: Academic Press, 2002. Second edition, 2006.

James, Judi. *Poker Face: Mastering Body Language to Bluff, Read Tells and Win*. New York: Marlowe and Company, 2007.

Knapp, Mark L., and Judith A. Hall. *Nonverbal Communication in Human Interaction*. Seventh edition. Florence: Wadsworth Publishing, 2009.

Lieberman, David J. *Never Be Lied to Again*. New York: St. Martin's Press, 1998.

———. *You Can Read Anyone: Never Be Fooled, Lied To, or Taken Advantage of Again*. Lakewood: Viter Press, 2007.

Liggett, John. *The Human Face*. London: Constable & Company Limited, 1974.

Lin, Henry B. *What Your Face Reveals: Chinese Secrets of Face Reading*. St. Paul: Llewellyn Publications, 1999.

Lip, Evelyn. *The Chinese Art of Face Reading*. Singapore: Times Books International, 1989. Revised edition published by Singapore: Marshall Cavendish International, 2009.

Marshall, Evan. *The Eyes Have It: Revealing Their Power, Messages, and Secrets*. New York: Citadel Press, 2003.

Mehrabian, Albert. *Silent Messages: Implicit Communication of Emotions and Attitudes*. Belmont: Wadsworth Publishing Company, 1971.

Meyer, Pamela. *Liespotting: Proven Techniques to Detect Deception*. New York: St. Martin's Press, 2010.

Miller, Gerald R., and James B. Stiff. *Deceptive Communication*. London: Sage Publications Limited, 1993.

Morris, Desmond. *Bodytalk: A World Guide to Gestures*. London: Jonathan Cape, 1994.

———. *Manwatching: A Field Guide to Human Behavior*. New York: Harry N. Abrams, 1977.

Navarro, Joe, with Marvin Karlins. *What Every Body is Saying: An Ex-FBI Agent's Guide to Speed-Reading People*. New York: HarperCollins, 2008.

Nierenberg, Gerald I., and Henry H. Calero. *How to Read a Person Like a Book*. New York: Pocket Books, 1971.

Pease, Allan, and Barbara Pease. *The Definitive Book of Body Language*. London: Orion Books Ltd., 2004.

Rosetree, Laura. *I Can Read Your Face*. Silver Spring: Aha! Experiences, 1988.

Rosetree, Rose. *The Power of Face Reading*. Sterling: Women's Intuition Worldwide, 2001.

Shea, Andy, and Steve Van Aperen. *The Truth About Lies: Uncovering the Fact from the Fiction*. Sydney, Australia: ABC Books, 2006.

Wainwright, Gordon R. *Master Body Language*. London: Hodder Education, 2011.

INDEX